CHAPLIN'S FILMS

South Brunswick and New York:
A. S. Barnes and Company

CHAPLIN'S
FILMS

UNO ASPLUND

translated from the Swedish by
Paul Britten Austin

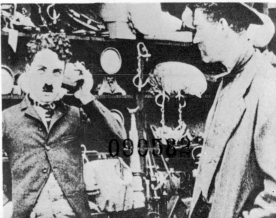

090582

© UNO ASPLUND 1971

Translation © PAUL BRITTEN AUSTIN 1973

Library of Congress Catalogue Card Number: 74-9308

A. S. Barnes and Company, Inc.
Cranbury, New Jersey 08512

First American edition 1976

ISBN 0-498-01604-8

PRINTED IN THE UNITED STATES OF AMERICA

Contents

090582

Foreword

A bowler, a walking stick, a moustache, a pair of outsize shoes—for the entire world these attributes signify but one man: Charlie Chaplin. Someone has pointed out the coincidence that Chaplin should be born in the same year as Edison invented the so-called Kinetoscope, that 'Peep-show for moving pictures' which was to be the embryo of the most modern of all media, the cinema. Unquestionably a coincidence, it nevertheless bears the hallmark of fate. By this invention Edison gave mankind its first glimpse of what was to become the magical world of movies—a world in which Chaplin, the genius of mime, was to be one of the greatest stars.

I do not intend to sit in judgment on Chaplin's art; nor shall I try to take the soundings of its profundity. Many others have already attempted that, and arrived at a variety of conclusions. My book is about Chaplin and his films. It examines in detail every film he has made starting with his earliest and least known period when he outlined the vagabond role that was to make him world-famous and, astonishingly enough, produced his greatest number of films.

If I have been able to do this it is because I have been so fortunate over the years, as to assemble good 8mm and 16mm copies of seventy-six of Chaplin's eighty-one films, including—with a single exception—all his silents. For years experts have been searching the extensive Chaplin literature for details of the footages and playing times of the fifty films Chaplin made for Keystone and Essanay in 1914–15.

I have also had access to the complete archives of Swedish and foreign films imported into Sweden which were first set up by the Swedish State in 1911, by an organisation which was also, less happily, to be the world's first film censor. The first copies of the earliest Chaplin films were registered on arrival in this archive, in all probability uncut. And there they are still to be seen. They give us a complete panorama of Chaplin's earliest work.

Another important aspect of my book, it seems to me, has been to present at some length details of Chaplin's most faithful and more important collaborators from the years of the silents; artistes who have been treated altogether too summarily in the Chaplin literature.

In the original Swedish edition of this book I have devoted a good deal of space to the activities and opinions of the Swedish censorship; and some of its utterances have been retained in the present edition. It should be pointed out as a matter of curiosity that even before 1920, and perhaps most of all then, Chaplin was so tremendous a favourite with Swedish film-goers that one can almost say his popularity was even greater in Sweden than in the USA! The only other country where it was perhaps comparable was France.

The reader may feel that there is too much statistical material. As I have worked on this book I have become more and more convinced that this information is important. It enriches the Chaplin literature and brings us closer to Chaplin himself and to his entourage of brilliant comedians.

I stand indebted to many, notably to *Statens Biografbyrå*, the State Film Archives in Stockholm, who have given me access to their material; and likewise to the Swedish Film Institute, which has contributed many valuable stills. Others have come from my own private collection.

My thanks also go to The National Film Archive, London, and to Mrs Eileen Bowser of the Museum of Modern Art, New York, for providing much valuable information. Similarly to the Danish Chaplin expert Karl J. Christensen, Copenhagen, who has been so kind as to contribute material about the Danish Board of Censors.

UNO ASPLUND

Chaplin's Profiles

Charlie Chaplin has broken all records in making people laugh. No one has so set a whole world laughing as the little man with the bowler hat, the cane and the overlarge shoes!

Much has been written about Chaplin's art and his legendary career, and opinions have varied widely. But perhaps the commentator who called him 'the most universal human being of our time' came closest to the truth. Those who have called him a genius stress the timeless and universally valid qualities in his work. It is an art fraught with tragic undertones and deeply human feeling, with which an audience cannot help but become involved and identified. It is for these reasons, I believe, that the figure of 'Charlie' has kept its grip on generation after generation.

All his biographers agree that Chaplin's miserable childhood in the London slums was the decisive influence in his development and in the type of films he made. Chaplin himself emphasises it in his memoirs. The more one reads about his earliest period, the more inclined one becomes to concur. And yet—there is something which does not *quite* fit. So pathetic an image seems a little diffuse and over-black. I cannot quite shake off the impression that on Chaplin's part there has been an unconscious 'dubbing' of the memories of childhood. For Chaplin, his suffering youth, bitter and harsh though it certainly was, has a lingering fascination; it gave him a world which he could transform with his imagination and project in stylised form on the silver screen.

When Chaplin writes in his memoirs 'I was well aware of the social stigma of our poverty', we must remember that up to his fifth year his parents, the music-hall artiste Hannah Chaplin and her artiste husband Charles, had been quite well-off. For a long while they had lived in a comfortable flat in Lambeth. Chaplin confirms that this was a time when he lived in 'a happy world'. Not until later, when his mother had separated from her bohemian and in the end dypsomaniac husband, did everything change. His mother lost her voice and thus her engagements and chance of earning a living. Finally, for long periods at a time, she was in a mental hospital. It was then that starvation stood at the door. It was then that Charlie and his brother Sydney were sent for a short while to the workhouse and that his time in a charity school and the struggle for daily bread brought Charlie into the slum milieu afterwards depicted by him in *The Kid*. But to claim that, for more than brief periods, he was chained to that world, is to put it too strongly. He chose to study it voluntarily in his spare time, devoting to it all the uninhibited curiosity and fascination of an over-gifted child. The addresses of the lodging houses where the family lived, with or without the mother, but always on the move, seem to indicate a lower middle-class rather than a slum milieu.

Always a hard worker, Chaplin and his half-brother (who was no less so) were not slow to fight their way out of their economic destitution. As early as the age of eight Chaplin had made a start in a small way in music hall, and by the turn of the century he was playing minor parts. Among other engagements, he went on tour for several years with a company which was playing *Sherlock Holmes*—Chaplin playing the part of Billy the bell-hop.

Chaplin's childhood experiences were unquestionably the powerful mainspring of his economic career and perhaps provided the origin of the rootlessness, introversion and lack of life-style and philosophy which he concedes are typical of him.

His tramp, whose roots go back to the *commedia dell'arte*, became a figure with whom people all over the world could identify. A simple little man of the people squeezed between giants, he never throws in the sponge and in the end often turns out to be the victor. Yet basically he is a tragic figure, not least on the emotional level. When it comes to competing for the favours of the fair sex, he is a washout—a theme discernible as early as the exquisite little poem from 1914, *The Face on the Bar Room Floor*, and which becomes even more explicit in *The Tramp* (1915), where the fully developed figure of the vagabond makes his first appearance, and recurs similarly in *The Vagabond* (1916) and *The Circus* (1928).

But Chaplin's social involvement, which was to become his leitmotif, belongs to a later phase. Little or no trace of it is to be found in his first year with Mack Sennett, the 'father of slapstick' and Chaplin's first employer in the cinema. What almost all his 1914 films do bear witness to, by contrast, is an uninhibited aggressiveness; a trait which certainly had its origins in music hall work with Fred Karno and which was unquestionably underplayed by Sennett, whose farces were always based on speed and action. If Chaplin found it hard to swallow Sennett's type of film, it certainly was not because of its tough action and sometimes fiercely sadistic elements and macabre endings, but because Sennett's insistence on high-speed action did not give him enough elbow-room for his own gags in which, by 1914, he had already begun to excel and which were afterwards to become his most brilliant hallmark. Not until the Mutual series (1916–17) did he find his style—a style which, even then, was not lacking in aggressive features.

Chaplin has never flinched from controversial subjects when they have appealed to his sense of commitment. To release a parody on war (*Shoulder Arms*) only a few weeks before the American troops came home from the hell of the trenches in the First World War (1918) was regarded as sheer lunacy. But the parody was received with rapture. So perfectly did it hit the nail on the head that even the homecoming soldiers found it irresistible and deeply appreciated this skit on what for them had been an all-too-grim reality.

Church-goers raged when Chaplin, in *The Pilgrim* (1923), one of his most surprising subjects, attacked non-conformist religiosity. But this time, too, the laugh was on his side. In *City Lights* (1931), it was the turn of capitalism. The image of the eccentric millionaire who had to get thoroughly tipsy in order to descend several steps of the social ladder and become human cannot have been all that easy for respectable audiences to digest.

Modern Times (1936) attacked the inhuman destructivity of the machine age. *The Great Dictator* (1940) caricatured Hitler and proclaimed Chaplin's view of world politics. In *Monsieur Verdoux* (1947) he stigmatises our modern society as a hothouse where the mentality of murderers thrives and flourishes. In *Limelight* (1952) he comes full circle; he is back in his youthful years in the London music hall world. It is Chaplin's emotional farewell to a vanished age. Once again he tells the story of Columbine and Pierrot, but seen now through the eyes of the lonely and ageing artiste whose beloved is forever out of reach and whose public has turned into a merciless mob.

And that was where Chaplin ought to have stopped. But America, for reasons best known to itself and deeply upset by his lack of diplomacy, had turned against him. Attacked by indignant and powerful women's associations, hunted down by the yellow press ruthlessness and the political vendetta of the McCarthy Age, he had been forced to retreat. From Europe he counterattacked in blind rage with *A King in New York* (1957), a film which, artistically speaking, ought never to have been made.

In many variants the figure of Charlie Chaplin has fought tyranny and injustice; it has never capitulated. If it has captured the whole world's interest it has been because Chaplin, thanks to his genius for satire and humour, has made his point in so liberating a manner. Bernard Shaw once declared: 'Chaplin is the only genius developed in motion pictures', an opinion in which the famous Irish playwright was certainly not alone.

There have of course been other great comedians. Why, then, has Chaplin been placed on so unique a pedestal? For my part I have nothing against reserving a niche for 'stony-faced' Buster Keaton. Yet the fact remains, Keaton never made such a hit or packed such a punch with the public as Chaplin. Only a later generation of cinéastes have discovered in Keaton too the qualities of a filmic genius. In the twenties Harold Lloyd enjoyed an even bigger following than Chaplin; but as a type, Lloyd's effete American mediocrity was a good deal more one-dimensioned. The same is true of 'babyface' Harry Langdon and of Fatty Arbuckle; Chaplin had a broader and deeper range.

But to return to our question—why should Chaplin, in particular, have got off to such a flying start? Perhaps because no one was better equipped than he to meet his public; and—above all—because he had the luck to meet it at the right moment, in the very years when the film was arriving in a big way as popular entertainment.

First and foremost, Chaplin was equipped with a lively and strong-willed intellect, which from the outset seethed with fertile ideas. In Fred Karno's English music hall shows he had taught himself the difficult art of mime and also that of the acrobat. Next, Mack Sennett put him through his hard and efficient school. With all these technical skills, Chaplin, sure of his own means of expression, was able almost from the start to break out of the usual farcical banalities. Slowly but surely he developed his vagabond—a vagabond who turned out to be at once simple and complex: simple in his way of giving pantomimic expression to his feelings in a variety of situations, but at the same time more than ambiguous in his behavioural patterns.

Charlie can be romantic and sentimental. He can be the nature-worshipper who, like Remarque's soldier trying to pluck a flower on the brink of the trenches, looks for wild flowers in the gutter. Yet in his youth he could also stand for that kind of brutal, almost sadistic, humour for which we today have less feeling. His excuse is that even then he was showing signs of his genius for mime.

If we remember his pathetic bread dance in *The Gold Rush* (1925), in which he so memorably dreams of escape from loneliness, we are also happy to recall all the times he has triggered off the huge spontaneous guffaw.

Of course the screen tramp and Chaplin the man have something in common. Yet there is something ambiguous about Chaplin's profile. Often he has assumed the image of an isolated, frequently temperamental and irritable artist, with overbearing traits, patriarchal by disposition. His memoirs unconsciously reveal his inferiority complex, one symptom of which seems to be his great weakness for rubbing shoulders with as many celebrities as possible. In words and photos he marshals them with the same uninhibited pride as a turn-of-the-century sports champion showing off his medals before the photographer.

In his films, too, he has dreamt various and grandiose dreams. In the twenties the press sometimes printed photos of Chaplin dressed up in Napoleon's uniform, glaring sombrely into the camera. Sam Goldwyn has spoken of Chaplin's interest in dictators and power. His film *The Great Dictator* depicted a neurotic Hitler and an overweening Mussolini. We can be sure his Napoleon, if he had ever played him, would not have been unreservedly received. But it was only one of many projects which came to nothing. Another ambition was to film 'the last of the cavaliers', Beau Brummel. (John Barrymore did it instead.) He similarly abandoned his plans for a serious satirical feature film, *Life* (1915).

Many writers have detected and emphasised Chaplin's search for perfection, a trait which over the years has sometimes led to controversies with his collaborators. This derives from the stupendous demands he has made both on himself and others.

Running parallel were his musical ambitions, which bloomed in the thirties. Before shooting *City Lights*, he devoted three months to special studies in the difficult art of composition, a new 'hobby' which so fascinated him that he even learnt how to conduct and while making the film mounted the podium. This, too, is a unique record: to unite in his person and in the same film the role of producer, director, actor, script-writer, composer and conductor! As a composer, naturally, Chaplin must only be judged as an enthusiastic gifted amateur. Yet even so great a melodist as Irving Berlin could only play the piano with one finger.

Chaplin's musical themes usually have a sentimental melodic line, easily identifiable as genuinely Chaplinesque, not least in the romantic waltz elements. The music dubbed on to *The Gold Rush* in 1942 is the best instance of his ability to underline the film drama musically. Though he had the help of arrangers, the music is unquestionably Chaplin's. 'Smile', from *Modern Times,* and the leitmotif of *Limelight* are among his authentic signature tunes; as authentic as 'This is my Song', in *A Countess from Hong Kong,* seems to be unauthentic, and a derivative from an earlier hit by Kiepura.

But whether or not they are consciously purloined—like 'La Violetera' in *City Lights* and the 'Cuff Song' in *Modern Times,* as well as many melodic elements from the classics, notably from Wagner—Chaplin's melodic contributions, from *City Lights* up to the latest synchronisation of *The Circus,* are an integral part of himself as a film-maker. In some way music has always been part and parcel of his means of expression.

Mime, involvement and imagination are the fundamentals of Chaplin's art. When the sound film arrived, he was the last to surrender. He thought it would be disastrous to his medium; all imagination would be lost. Not until 1940 and *The Great Dictator* did he bow to the demands of the age.

If we look at him merely as a *director,* on the other hand, his work seems more hum-drum. Some of his shorter films show signs of true originality, for example, certain camera angles in *The Tramp* and the tracking shot used in *Easy Street.* As a director he was unquestionably most successful in *A Woman of Paris* (1923), whose railway scene with fluttering shadowy faces illustrating a passing train is one of those little details of film directing that have become historic. Otherwise one can hardly claim that Chaplin has been much interested in camera work, or in the possibility of décor and montage. It has always been the artistic shaping of his Charlie figure which has been the dominant element. *A Countess from Hong Kong* (1967) made in the autumn of his days, speaks volumes about the inevitable shortcomings of a unique all-rounder.

From artistic matters to material ones: Charlie Chaplin has been one of the few happy mortals who, from the very outset of their career, have been able to make a vast fortune—and keep it.

His salary curve as a film star on contract is virtually unique—figures, we should note, valid for a period fifty years ago, when money was worth a great deal more than it is today and taxes in the USA were as moderate as could be! *1913*: 50 dollars a week with Fred Karno; *1914*: 175 dollars with Mack Sennett; *1915*: 1,250 dollars with Essanay; *1916–17*: 10,000 dollars with Mutual (plus a transfer fee of 150,000 dollars!); and finally *1918*: a million-dollar contract with First National for nine films over a period of eighteen months. As an oddity we may note that during his years with Mutual Chaplin earned an average of $667,000 while the salary of the President of the United States was only one seventh of that figure!

How could the management pay out such stupendous sums? The fact is they had to. Competition for the star was fierce and Chaplin was always receiving new offers. The studios had realised how the crowds flocked to his films. It was calculated a few years ago that each of Chaplin's films had been seen by some 350 million people. From 1914–23 a cinema in New York, The Crystal Hall on 14th Street, showed nothing but Chaplin films. No film star has ever had a bigger public, and hardly any other star has stayed at the top so long.

But all medals have their obverse. In Chaplin's case it has been a stormy private life, full of marital mix-ups, scandals and campaigns of political persecution. All this of course has left its traces, even in his harmonious old age, as we see from what he has to say in his memoirs about 'my evil destinies'; but also in his summing up: 'I have been cosseted in the world's affections, loved and hated.'

Important biographical data

Born in London, 16 April, 1889 in East Lane, Walworth, parents Charles and Hannah Chaplin, both music hall artistes

First appearance before a camera, 1896 when, aged seven, placed himself in front of a newsreel cameraman filming the Scots Guards as they marched through St James's Park, London

First stage appearance when, aged eight, toured the provinces in a musical called *The Eight Lancaster Lads*. (That is, if we overlook the improvised appearance aged five, when he sang a song one evening in variety, after his mother had been taken ill)

Second stage appearance, 15 January 1900, in *Giddy Ostende* at the Hippodrome Theatre, London

Member of Fred Karno's famous English vaudeville troupe from 1906 to 1913

First American stage appearance, 3 October 1910, in the vaudeville *The Wow Wows* at the Colonial Theatre, New York, during the Karno troupe's tour

Mack Sennett, contract with, from 29 November 1913

Hollywood, arrived in early December 1913

First film, with Keystone (Mack Sennett) in the one-reel *Making a Living*; première, 2 February 1914

35 films, mostly one-reels, with Mack Sennett, in 1914

Essanay Company, transfers to in 1915. From February 1916 on, makes 14 films, plus the materials for a 'bogus' fifteenth

Makes his breakthrough with the Mutual Company 1916–17, where he completes his famous suite of 12 two-reelers

First National, transfers to in 1918, and therewith a series of longer and more advanced films

First marriage (to the sixteen-year-old film actress Mildred Harris), 1918. Divorced in 1920. One son born in this marriage, but died after a day or so

United Artists formed in 1919, with the quartet of stars Charlie Chaplin, Douglas Fairbanks, Mary Pickford and the director David W. Griffith on the board

First full-length feature film directed by himself, *The Kid,* released in 1921

Journey to Europe, 1921, becomes a triumphal progress and gives him new contacts and ideas for films; also his first book *My Trip Abroad*

Chaplin's first film for United Artists, A Woman of Paris, completed in 1923, in which Chaplin for the first time tackles the directing alone, and for the first time also is entirely independent as producer

Second marriage 1924, to sixteen-year-old Lita Grey, who bears him two sons, Charles Spencer and Sydney Earle, before their divorce is made public in 1927

Special Award at the first Oscar Prize-giving, 1929, for 'versatility and genius in writing, acting, directing and producing *The Circus'*

Third marriage (kept secret for several years) to the film star Paulette Goddard 1933—the couple separated in 1942

First talkie, The Great Dictator, 1940. (*Modern Times,* 1936, with its musical illustrations and its brief song sequence is usually classified as a silent)

The scandal case (1943–4) in which Chaplin is unjustly accused of being the father of the child of a film-struck girl, Joan Barry. Great sensation in the USA, bruited widely by the American press

Fourth marriage 1943 to Oona O'Neill, daughter of Nobel Prize-winning playwright Eugene O'Neill. By her Chaplin has eight children, of these the eldest daughter Geraldine has made her own career in films

Chaplin leaves USA 17 September 1952, 39 years after his début with Mack Sennett—tired of all the political and moralistic controversies with the authorities and threatened by the tax gatherers. He settles in Switzerland at the Manoir de Ban in the village of Corsier just outside Vevey, where he has since lived

Last film made in USA, *Limelight,* 1952

Last film in which Chaplin has played the lead, *A King in New York,* shot in London, première 1957

His memoirs, entitled *My Autobiography,* published 1964

Directs the film *A Countess from Hong Kong,* 1967

Preparations for his eightysecond film, *The Freak* began 1969 but so far (1973) have not led to any results

Reconciliation with USA in April 1972, when Chaplin was invited to Hollywood to receive an Oscar statuette for his unique contributions to the film industry. Rapturously acclaimed, beyond anything so far known in the history of the Oscar

Competitors and Imitators

There is a good story of how, some time prior to the twenties, Charlie Chaplin—whose tramp was already a widely known and beloved figure—entered a competition, incognito, for who could best mimic the great film idol. And came fifth! True or not, it is a fact that imitators were not slow to seize on the Charlie figure. They tried to imitate his walk, his clothes, his behaviour—and make money out of it. All too often they succeeded.

But if many people borrowed from Chaplin, there is no doubt but that he alone created the essence of the figure from study of the English variety artistes who were appearing on unpretentious London stages around the turn of the century. Even at an early age he was paying close heed to details. As an eight-year-old he had a chance to appear as a cat in a Christmas pantomime, playing against Marceline, a celebrated clown. In his memoirs he relates how he aroused the audience's delight and the producer's wrath by lifting his leg, dog-wise, against the proscenium. The theme recurs with variations in his films. The gentlemanly tramp who, having trodden in dog-muck, scrapes his sole with his walking stick and then polishes his nails on it, was certainly another gag inspired by the vaudeville stage.

During Chaplin's London days there had been an English variety artiste, Little Tich, who used to wear the same outsize shoes on the stage and in short films. Chaplin must have seen him. Even more influential was another variety star, Fred Kitchen (1873–1951), one of Fred Karno's company. It was he who, according to a statement by Peter Coates and Thelma Niklaus in *The Little Fellow*, took the newcomer under his wing and gave him his first lessons in mime for Karno.

Whether or not this is so—in his memoirs Chaplin himself only mentions Kitchen in passing as a 'fine artiste'—he has never denied being influenced by and learning from the French pioneer come-

18

dian Max Linder, who was born in 1885 and had begun filming as early as 1905. Chaplin first saw Linder's films during a visit to Paris with Karno in 1909. How deeply he appreciated him can be judged from a photo he donated to Linder, long afterwards, inscribed: 'To the one and only Max, "the Professor", from his disciple Charlie Chaplin.' But by then Chaplin was already the great star and Linder was on his way out after an unsuccessful stay in the USA. He committed suicide in tragic circumstances in 1925.

In view of the enormous popularity of the Chaplin films in the USA as early as late 1914 (his first year with Mack Sennett) it is easy to be beguiled into thinking that Chaplin was already in a class by himself. Nothing could be less true.

In 1914 he had at least one equal, or even superior, in the public's affection: the ebullient John Bunny (1863–1915). Bunny who had only begun his career at the age of forty-seven in 1910, swiftly achieved unbelievable popularity. In the years 1912–14 he played in more than 150 one- and two-reelers, most of them against Flora Finch. As a type, Bunny was a good natured fellow with a figure outclassing even 'Fatty' Arbuckle's.

'Fatty' (1887-1932) whose real Christian name was Roscoe, was another serious rival. He appeared in six films with Chaplin during the Keystone period. When, in 1913, Chaplin made his modest entrée in the studio, Arbuckle was at the top of his form with Mack Sennett playing with, among others, Mabel Norman.

Chaplin had other rivals nearer to home. The Scotsman Billie Ritchie (1877–1921), the Russian born Billy West and, to a lesser extent, the Englishman Billy Reeves (d 1945), made a trio of artistes living well on imitating Charlie. Ritchie even went so far as to declare that it was Chaplin who had imitated *him* when he designed his tramp! Of the three, West was without question the most industrious and adept plagiarist. In 1919, among other films, he made *Hey Police*, strongly resembling Chaplin's *Police* and including the entire scene in which Chaplin and his chum break into a private house. Among West's other 'Chaplin films' around the years 1911–16 can be mentioned *The Hobo, His Day Out, The Rogue, The Chief Cook*, and the series about Charlie, which were presented abroad as vaguely Chaplin films, sometimes even with the Charlie figure in the advertisements. (See Chapter 11 on spurious Chaplin films.) West often played opposite the afterwards celebrated Oliver Hardy, unquestionably a conscious combination *á la* Chaplin, and with the massive Eric Campbell and Mack Swain.

But to return to Chaplin and his popularity. In 1915, when Chaplin was bought over by Essanay and had begun to be exported all over the world, he was still meeting with stiff competition. As a curiosity it may be mentioned that, in a big popularity poll in Britain that year, he came no higher than third. During the next few years, though he became a 'name' in Sweden in the autumn of 1915, Fatty and Linder went on drawing equally big audiences, and Billie Ritchie and Billy West, as I have said, were being presented in popular films under the name of Chaplin.

Ritchie's release of a plagiary of the same name was certainly inspired by Chaplin's first full-length feature film *Tillie's Punctured Romance* (1914). Many of the filmgoers who watched it in 1915 were certainly under the misapprehension that they were seeing Chaplin. Ritchie's film *The Big Spring Fly* was advertised in the Stockholm newspapers with the same original block which two years earlier had been used to introduce Chaplin in the Swedish trade press! On 12 November 1917 one Stockholm cinema (The Chicago) advertised 'Charlie Chaplin in *Cold Hearts and Heat Flames*'. But the lead was taken by Billie Ritchie, who here courted the daughter of a hotelier. By this time Chaplin himself, however, had begun to win an established reputation with the Swedish public, his popularity reaching a climax in the years 1918–20. But then came two other comedians who seriously threatened his position. Harold Lloyd, the American good boy in his lenseless spectacles; and 'stony face' Buster Keaton.

Harold Lloyd's name first appeared in the Swedish press on 14 April 1919, when his one-reeler had its première in Stockholm. Ten or so one-reelers were later released in Sweden in 1919 and he was advertised as 'Chaplin's dangerous new rival'. Lloyd's first figure before his 'spectacle' period, Willie Work, though one cannot claim that it was a direct plagiary of Chaplin, was based on his tramp.

By 1920 Lloyd had firmly established himself in the favours of the Swedish public, whom he treated to twenty-five first nights, mostly one-reelers. Chaplin had a rival of his own stature. A few years later even in the USA Harold had overtaken him as a box office draw.

Buster Keaton, on the other hand, though he appeared in the Swedish movie repertoire in the same year as Lloyd (1919), played against Fatty Arbuckle in the main role in ten two-reelers. Not until 1921 did Buster Keaton acquire a profile of his own in a series of one-reelers. Only from 1923 onwards was he in a position to challenge Chaplin and Lloyd in ever more extensive farces.

So Chaplin had plenty of rivals tramping on his heels—not to mention a certain Mexican actor, Charles Amador, who rechristened himself Charles Aplin, and the German imitator who called himself Charlie Kaplin. Chaplin sued the former in 1924, but did not bother himself about the latter.

The lawsuit against Charles Amador, in Los Angeles, repays study, as it concerned the question of artistic copyright on an established figure in the movies, in this case 'Charlie'. Not only had Amador adopted the tramp's outer attributes, the moustache, the bowler, the big shoes, the tight jacket and baggy trousers; he had come as close as he could to adopting Chaplin's surname with intent to deceive the public. This was going a step too far. Chaplin intervened after Amador had begun the production of a series of films for a minor American company, Western Feature Productions.

During the suit, Amador's lawyer maintained that the figure of Charlie was not original. He had done an incredible amount of research into the origins of the tramp outfit, and had come to the following conclusions. The typical moustache had been worn in 1899 by George Behan playing the part of a French waiter on a Chicago stage. In 1898, a certain Chris Lane had played in the variety show in the same sort of hat. Several comedians, the lawyer pointed out, had used the typical Chaplinesque way of walking as early as 1892. Further he maintained that, since 1908, Billie Reeves had been wearing the same baggy trousers and behaving in the same manner as Chaplin's figure; and that Billie Ritchie (as the latter himself had intimated) had appeared in the Charlie outfit both on the stage and in films before Chaplin had become well-known.

But this line of argument collapsed. Reeves' own brother, who had been a good friend of Ritchie's—by the time of the lawsuit Ritchie had died—came forward and told the court that both Ritchie and Reeves had intentionally been imitating Chaplin and that they had neither worn the tramp outfit nor used his typical gestures before Chaplin. The verdict went in Chaplin's favour, and Mr Amador had to inhibit the rest of his 'Chaplin series'.

Chaplin has had many imitators on the stage as well as in films. The best performers of Chaplin sketches, in my view, have been the world-famous clown Charlie Rivels in his 'Chaplain on the Trapeze' number, and the Danish comedienne-pianist, Claire Feldern, with her exquisite musical parody. Another famous TV comedienne, Lucille Ball, has also imitated Charlie the Tramp with a certain degree of success. But the original is, and will remain, beyond the grasp of other artists.

Chaplin and the Censors

Chaplin has had many a brush with the film censors. Here again my own country, Sweden, affords a good instance. The Swedish Board of Film Censors is the oldest in the world. It began operations in December 1911, under state control, having been set up in order to cope with the multifarious flora of films blooming in Sweden in the first decade of the century—and which had come to provoke protests from the representatives of public morals. They were demanding a clean-up.

One of its first victims was Charlie Chaplin. The first time this happened was on 12 November 1914, when Svenska Biografteatern submitted the first Chaplin film to find its way to the freezing north: a copy of *Mabel's Married Life*. The main figure, rechristened in Swedish 'Dille Krog'—more or less Dither Pub—was played by Chaplin. The censors' horror and disgust can be read in their account of the film's contents.

'The filthy Mr Dille Krog gets drunk. His wife gets herself a mannequin to box with. When he gets home Dille Krog takes the mannequin to be a rival and starts a fight. Finally Mrs Krog explains what it's all about and Dille is reconciled to her.' Final verdict: 'Brutalising, singularly tasteless and simple-minded.'

The Swedish censors were happily unaware that at the same time the American press was praising the film, saying that 'the audience was shaken with laughter' and finding that Chaplin had made an admirable study of a drunk. Not that this differing opinion would have changed theirs.

The distributors however, were optimists. After four years they tried again; but despite a new title, 'Charlie's Rival', the censors were on the alert. Their description of the film's contents this time were a trifle more sober, but the epithet 'brutalising' remained. The film remained banned until 1970, when a new copy was released—a U-certificate, naturally!—fifty-six years after the film had first arrived in Sweden!

090582

Another film which fell under the censors' ban—three times over—was *Caught in the Rain*, also made in 1914 by Mack Sennett. This time the censors were even more indignant. They summarised: 'Charlie flirts with a married woman and goes to the same hotel where she and her husband are staying. Undressed, he is lying in bed when the married woman, equally undressed and walking in her sleep, comes in to him and joins him in bed. After various adventures thus lightly costumed, they sink down together.'

The whole film was about as innocent as could be and certainly no masterpiece of the art of farce. But such was not the approved language of love in those days. The censors were crying wolf. This film, too, was reprieved in 1970.

The third film born under an unlucky star (as far as Sweden was concerned) was *Mabel's Strange Predicament*, the first in which Chaplin played against Mabel Normand. Here, too, 'daring' bedroom scenes brought down the curtain. The film has in fact never been shown in the Swedish repertoire.

Lastly, *Those Love Pangs*, too, was stopped. Here is how the censors described it: 'Charlie and another shabbily dressed man, whose trousers seem ready to fall off at any moment, are rivals for a girl. After the introductory scene with a rotten egg Charlie stabs his rival in the buttock with a fork, and the latter does the same to Charlie. Afterwards we see Charlie, who is courting two ladies at once and mainly expressing his feelings with his legs, throw a rival into the lake. Finally Charlie gets flung through a sheet of paper (actually a film screen). A number of fight scenes form part of the action.'

One more quotation is worth rescuing from oblivion. In *A Night Out* Chaplin played against the cross-eyed Ben Turpin. The film contains a scene which has made latter-day Chaplin chroniclers fall into raptures: 'what subtle poetry did he not genially express when, dragged along the street by his mate, he plucks a flower in the gutter...'

But the censors had no feeling for this sort of poetry. We read on the card: 'Chaplin and his friend appear badly drunk in an hotel, his friend drags the drunken Charlie along the street, Charlie kicks and struggles—among other things he kicks a lady in the lower part of her back—and in his night attire gets into calamitous situations with a married woman, also dressed for the night. Finally Chaplin ends up in a bathtub. Totally forbidden.' (Ban lifted in 1930.) No, the tough Charlie of 1914 vintage found no mercy with the Swedish authorities. And in a way, one can understand.

If we continue our researches in the impressive heap of censors' statements which the Swedish Board of Film Censors have so kindly placed at the author's disposal, we find altogether 31 white cards (white meaning totally banned) in their collection. This however did not mean that Swedes were deprived of a chance to see thirty-one Chaplin films, it was not as bad as all that. Yet altogether twenty-one were banned once or more times, and of these eighteen were subsequently released after the distributors had renewed their applications. Two films long withheld from the public were *Laughing Gas* and *The Rounders*. They joined the repertoire only in 1955.

Many odd things occurred. *Tillie's Punctured Romance*—Chaplin's first full-length film (1914)—was totally banned in 1919, only to be approved, *even for children*, in 1920. But when a new copy, 200 metres shorter—was submitted in 1924 the film was given an A certificate! Incomprehensible.

Odd, too, but logical, was the fate of *The New Janitor*. On a first viewing in 1916 it was released, even for children, but when it came back in 1920 was totally banned. The reason was simple. In this film a burglar breaks into a house, but the heroic janitor (Charlie), who is hopelessly in love with a pretty office girl, takes the thief by surprise after he has seized the cash till, and proves more than a match for him, ending up with the girl. The explanation was that the copy submitted by the importer in 1920 lacked its happy ending. In it the thief manages to make off with the cash till—and we never see him caught. It was this the censor disliked. For crime to pay was immoral, and must not be permitted. And so the verdict was a white card which read: 'Confuses notions of right and wrong by having no ending. The burglar escapes scot free.'

Other 'indecent' actions were frowned upon. From the film *A Film Johnny* (1919) we note: 'A section cut in which Chaplin lifts his leg *à la* dog.' And from *The Property Man* (1918) 'Cut where Chaplin demonstrates that he has wetted his pants.' From *Getting Acquainted* (1917) the shots 'in which Charlie with the hook of his walking stick lifts Mabel's skirt' were cut out. Likewise the 'section where, with the crook of his walking stick, he pulls over the constable.' Mack Sennett might be allowed to poke fun at his policemen, but there had to be measure in all things . . .

More easily understandable to us are the ravages made by the censor in *Mabel at the Wheel* (1915) and his remark: 'The stone-throwing scene where the man shut up in the shed is whipped and Mabel bites Chaplin's hand, has been removed.'

Altogether, brick-throwings were popular ingredients in Chaplin's first films. They contributed to the premature ends of a number of actors, and some actresses.

A rather unique aspect of the censors' job was to teach script-writers to use more respectful language. In the film *Caught in a Cabaret* (1919) there is a scene where one of the gentry's servants apologises that their eminent guest has still not arrived. The censor points out: 'The text "The Minister is late" ought to be changed to "The Minister is delayed".' No one has time for such subleties today.

This run-through of the Swedish censors' activities has been invaluable in helping me to map out Chaplin's early films in detail. A register was kept of the lengths of films both before and after cutting, and an indication of their contents, so that it has often been possible to identify films under mysterious titles. In the collection, before the present author sorted them out, were no fewer than 326 titles, including 26 cavalcades and 34 spurious Chaplin films.

This, however, is by no means a unique state of affairs in Chaplin's output. In British and American lists down the years I have noted altogether 214 titles of 81 films! If all the reduction print versions were included, the list would be infinitely longer. In French, alone, there are at least 170 titles, most of them of course from the 'jungle' years 1914–15. The same also applies in high degree to the Swedish collection.

All this makes one feel like appealing to importers and cinema owners all over the world for the future to do their best to sort out the Chaplin materials, not to send out unduly cut copies (even to matinées), and always to provide them with their accepted original titles.

It may be true that the earliest Chaplin films are of purely historical interest. But from the public's point of view and for reasons of mere decency the least one can ask is that such of the older films as are shown commercially should be released in copies *more or less* of original length and *reasonably good quality*. So much, at least, we owe to Chaplin. This is a rule which should apply to all old-timers. That the old silents, for technical reasons, cannot be run at the correct speed is much to be regretted; but there is nothing we can do about it. The stock of such films is going to shrink steadily as time passes and they become more difficult to come by. Every care must be taken.

The Keystone Period

My filmography of Charlie Chaplin's eighty-one films is based in the first instance on material from my own film library, complemented with information from Chaplin students in other countries.

The lists of actors and foreign titles have been established on the basis of material by Theodore Huff, Jean Mitry and Gerald D. McDonald, Michael Conway and Marc Ricci. To this I have added a good deal that is my own, as well as making sizeable corrections, both concerning the roles and the actors who played them.

Mack Sennett's primitive Keystone Studios were situated at Glendale, California, address 1712 Alesandro Street. Here, since the summer of 1912, 'the father of slapstick' had been presiding over his famous group of farce comedians led by Mabel Normand, Ford Sterling, Fatty Arbuckle, Mack Swain and Chester Conklin. And here one-reelers and half-reelers were being shot in quick succession, often two films alternately on the same set.

Though Chaplin arrived in early December 1913, he long remained 'out of work'. He was regarded as an oddity, and Sennett could not really figure out how he ought to use him. Not until around the new year under one of Sennett's directors, Henry 'Pathé' Lehrman, was the young music-hall actor, aged 24, given a chance to show his talents. However, the shooting was marred by a clash of wills. It was hardly the start in films for which Chaplin had been hoping.

1   Making a Living (1 reel)

FIRST NIGHT 2 Feb 1914
ALTERNATIVE TITLES A Busted Johnny, Troubles, Doing his Best

MAIN FRENCH TITLE Pour Gagner sa Vie
DIRECTOR Henry Lehrman
CAMERAMAN E. J. Vallejo
ACTORS Chaplin (reporter), Henry Lehrman (reporter),
Virginia Kirtley (girl), Alice Davenport (her mother),
Minta Durfee (flirtatious girl), Chester Conklin (policeman
and tramp)

Chaplin, dressed in a grey frock coat and top hat and wearing a
walrus moustache and monocle—all drawn from his stage roles
with Fred Karno—plays the part of a swindler. At the beginning
of the film he is chatting up a mother and her daughter, and
becomes involved in a wild struggle with the latter's fiancé, a press
photographer, who has been naive enough to lend him some money.

Chaplin, broke, is obliged to find himself a job and accepts an
offer as a newspaper reporter. He witnesses a car accident, in which
a car runs over a cliff. His rival has snapped the scene, but Chaplin
grabs the camera and rushes off to the editorial office, chased by his
rival and a policeman. During this chase his rival gets stuck in the
bedroom of an unknown lady and is exposed to her husband's
jealousy. Chaplin gets to the editorial office and is received with
open arms as he hands in 'his' scoop.

Just to make sure, he personally supervises the distribution of
the newspaper. But then his rival turns up and again begins chasing
him through the town. Their final scuffle ends indecisively on the
cow-catcher of a streetcar.

Chaplin was far from pleased with his first appearance in films.
In his view, Lehrman had ruined it by cutting down many well
worked out gags. What Sennett wanted above all was tempo.
Nothing was allowed to hold up the action. Thus all the finest
nuances were lost. For the first but not the last time two farce-styles
had clashed in the Keystone studios.

Sennett too was dissatisfied with this film; but the public liked
it. Critics praised the anonymous actor and *Moving Picture World*
called him 'a comedian of the first water'.

2   Kid Auto Races at Venice (split reel)

FIRST NIGHT 8 Feb 1914
ALTERNATIVE TITLE The Children's Automobile Race
MAIN FRENCH TITLE Charlot est Content de Lui
DIRECTOR Henry Lehrman

CAMERAMAN Frank D. Williams (NB Since virtually all
Chaplin's Keystone films were filmed by Williams his name
as cameraman will hereafter be omitted)
ACTORS Chaplin (in his 'tramp' outfit for the first time),
Henry Lehrman (the film director), The Keystone Kids, in
minor roles on the racetrack (Billy Jacobs, Thelma Salter,
Gordon Griffith, Charlotte Fitzpatrick)

Chaplin's second film has hardly any action to speak of. Sennett
had heard that a baby-cart race was to be held at Venice, a seaside
resort near Los Angeles, and sent Henry Lehrman out there to
exploit the popular occasion. Chaplin was told to borrow the
materials for a funny costume from his comrades, and by pure
chance it was here that the world-famous Charlie outfit was born.
The overlarge trousers were contributed by Fatty Arbuckle, the
outsize shoes belonged to Ford Sterling and for good measure were
worn on the wrong foot; the bowler—a couple of sizes too small—
belonged to the father of Minta Durfee (one of Sennett's ladies and
married to Fatty). Finally, the moustaches were borrowed from
Mack Swain and cut down to Hitler size. This costume crystallised
the tramp character that had been forming in Chaplin's mind.

In an interview (1923) he afterwards gave his own version of the
symbolism of Charlie's costume:

His little moustache? That is a symbol of vanity. His skimpy coat,
his trousers so ridiculously baggy and shapeless? They are the
caricature of our eccentricity, our stupidities, our clumsiness. The
idea of the walking-stick was perhaps my happiest inspiration, for
the cane was what made me speedily known. Moreover, I developed
business with it to such a point that it took on a comic character
of its own. Often I found it hooked round someone's leg, or
catching him by the shoulder, and in these ways I got a laugh from
the public while I was myself scarcely aware of the gesture. I don't
think I had fully understood in the beginning how much, among
millions of individuals, a walking-stick puts a label marked 'dandy'
on a man. So that when I waddled on to the stage with my little
walking-stick and a serious air, I gave the impression of an attempt
at dignity, which was exactly my aim.

Chaplin can hardly have thought the matter through so thoroughly in 1914 when he was ordered on to the race track and
instructed to cause as much trouble as he could, to get in the way
of the 'false' cameraman (Lehrman himself), cause confusion on
the track, and in general irritate both functionaries and public. He
succeeded—to say the least of it. The closeups of Chaplin are noteworthy; especially so since closeups were unusual at that time.

28

The whole film is said to have taken no more than forty-five minutes to shoot. Running time was about eleven minutes, ie about a quarter of the shooting time—unquestionably a world record in film history. In its improvised character this little farce is typical of Mack Sennett's way of going to work. He utilised an authentic milieu and event, got the public and authorities to join in—free—and made money on the results. The script, if there was one, was a secondary matter.

3 Mabel's Strange Predicament (1 reel)

FIRST NIGHT 9 Feb 1914
ALTERNATIVE TITLE Hotel Mixup
MAIN FRENCH TITLE L'Étrange Adventure de Mabel
DIRECTORS Henry Lehrman and Mack Sennett
ACTORS Chaplin, Mabel Normand, Harry McCoy, Alice
Davenport, Hank Mann, Chester Conklin, Al St John

The action takes place in a hotel foyer, where a somewhat tipsy Chaplin makes his entry in a series of ingenious misadventures. He bumps into—and is fascinated by—the elegant lady (Mabel Normand), gets entangled in her dog's leash and falls on his face, all without losing his dignity. He tries to make a call over an automatic telephone but lacks the necessary nickel, and causes confusion among the hotel staff.

Later he runs into Mabel in the hotel corridor, where she is playing with her dog and has got locked out of her room. This is followed by a confused chase through various rooms, Mabel ending up in that of an elderly husband where she hides under the bed. The man's jealous wife intervenes, and so does Mabel's admirer (Harry McCoy) and the uninvited guest Charlie gets all the knocks in the hullaballoo; then the time is ripe for a happy ending between Mabel and her admirer.

In his memoirs Chaplin's memory has failed him in associating his vagabond costume with this film. Several eye-witnesses, among them Chester Conklin and Minta Durfee, confirm that the outfit had its origin in *Kid Auto Races at Venice*, which was made before Mabel Normand's first appearance in a Chaplin picture. But the two films were premièred on successive days. While *Mabel's Strange Predicament* was *prepared* before *Kid Auto Races*, the brief racing film was interpolated because the opportunity suddenly offered itself.

This film, Chaplin's third, was the first—in point of date of production—to be totally banned by the Swedish censors and was never shown in Sweden. Why? The censors' card tells us: 'Brutalising. Chaplin, a hotel guest, gets mixed up in a series of amorous complications, some of which are of the most tasteless sort, eg, rubs cheeks in scenes of jealousy where lovers are caught in the act.'

The American press thought otherwise. The critic who wrote of this film in *Exhibitor's Mail* showed quite fantastic foresight when he wrote that within six months Chaplin would be one of the world's most popular comedians. In America, indeed, it took even less time before his fame was a reality.

4   Between Showers (1 reel)

FIRST NIGHT 28 Feb 1914
ALTERNATIVE TITLES The Flirts, Charlie and the Umbrella,
In Wrong
MAIN FRENCH TITLE Charlot et la Parapluie
DIRECTOR Henry Lehrman
ACTORS Chaplin, Ford Sterling (his rival), Emma Clifton
(object of their passion), Chester Conklin (policeman),
Sadie Lampe

Between Showers was the last Chaplin film to be directed by Henry Lehrman. It is an episode in rainy weather, in which there is a struggle over an umbrella. Ford Sterling and Chaplin compete in showing politeness toward a young lady (Emma Clifton) who is vainly trying to cross a muddy street. Sterling fetches a plank which Chaplin grabs from him, and there is a struggle over Sterling's umbrella. The policeman (Chester Conklin) is summoned and resolves the dispute after an innocent tramp has been pushed into the lake during the rivals' fight. The lady leaves Charlie, Charlie hands over the umbrella and the policeman arrests the trouble-maker Sterling. At the beginning of the film the policeman flirts briefly but intensively with another young lady (Sadie Lampe).

Already Chaplin is beginning to find his form as Charlie. In this film it is interesting to study his playing against the Keystone star Ford Sterling, who here develops his characteristic pattern of movements, including an original way of running with convulsive hops and flexed knees. It was both the first and last time that these two were paired. Sterling left Keystone in February 1914, not—as many have averred—because he felt outclassed by Chaplin, but because he felt that he was getting too little money. Up to 1914 he had been Mack Sennett's great star. He had already left when the first Chaplin films began to come out.

Sterling accepted an offer from the famous producer Carl Laemmle, but later went back to Mack Sennett, who had by then lost Chaplin.

5   A Film Johnny (1 reel)

FIRST NIGHT 2 March 1914
ALTERNATIVE TITLES Movie Nut, Million Dollar Job,
Charlie at the Studio
MAIN FRENCH TITLE Charlot Fait du Cinéma
DIRECTOR Mack Sennett
ACTORS Chaplin, Virginia Kirtley, Fatty Arbuckle,
Minta Durfee, The Keystone Cops

Many Chaplin films show us what a film studio looked like at the beginning of the century, eg, in *The Masquerader, His New Job* and *Behind the Screen*. The first of such films is *A Film Johnny*.

Charlie, enamoured of the cinema, goes to see a film and on the screen sees a girl whom he falls for and at all costs wants to meet. To look for her he goes to the Keystone Studios, where he causes a commotion during a film shooting. Fire breaks out. Charlie is blamed for its ravages and not only gets squirted by the fire brigade but is given the push by the beautiful prima donna. The funniest scene is the one in which Charlie, squirted by the fire brigade, wrings out his ears and squirts back.

6   Tango Tangles (1 reel)

FIRST NIGHT 9 March 1914
ALTERNATIVE TITLES Charlie's Recreation, Music Hall
MAIN FRENCH TITLE Charlot Danseur
DIRECTOR Mack Sennett
ACTORS Chaplin, Ford Sterling (band leader), Fatty Arbuckle
(member of the orchestra), Minta Durfee (wardrobe keeper),
Chester Conklin

Chaplin has abandoned his typical costume, appearing as a smooth-shaven young dandy who in a rather tipsy condition visits a dance hall. In 1914 dancing was all the rage in the USA and a Music Hall therefore became a suitable setting for Mack Sennett to use.

Around the pretty wardrobe girl (Minta Durfee) have gathered three admirers: the band leader (Ford Sterling), who regards himself as engaged to her, another member of the orchestra (Fatty Arbuckle) and Chaplin. The latter's unremitting attentions to her on the dance floor irritate his rivals, more especially the fiancé, who starts a fight with Chaplin.

The end is chaos, both the champions being counted out unconscious. A demonstration dance by a pair of professional dancers opens the film in order to give it the right atmosphere.

7   His Favourite Pastime (1 reel)

FIRST NIGHT 16 March 1914
ALTERNATIVE TITLES The Bonehead, Reckless Fling
MAIN FRENCH TITLE Charlot entre le Bar et l'Amour
DIRECTOR George Nichols
ACTORS Chaplin (steady customer), Fatty Arbuckle (another client), Peggy Pearce (beautiful lady)

This is the prototype of the 'unpleasant' tough films of which so many are found in Chaplin's 1914 output. It is hardly surprising that the censor was horrified at this story of the ravages of a drunken bar-lounger. Charlie starts it off with a hullaballoo at the bar, where he fights the other clients and has a controversy with a swing door—which was to have many successors. The scene in which he finally gives up and crawls out *under* it is funny.

Having had enough to drink he follows by streetcar the beautiful lady, who has taken a taxi, and then breaks into her home. Among other things he pays his attentions to a coloured maid but discovers that she is not the one he is looking for, and is thrown out. One of the crueller jokes is when a negro waiter asks for a tip and a burning match is put into his hand instead. The film ends with a full-scale fight when the master of the household comes home and finds Charlie trying to seduce his wife. Fatty Arbuckle is in the film, not as the husband—as British film historians have maintained—but as the ragged drinker in the bar, Charlie's first victim.

The American critics of 1914 were, oddly enough, delighted. What are we to say about *Motion Picture News*: 'If there is an audience anywhere that does not roar when they see this comedy they cannot be in the full possession of their wits.' Chaplin's fan-

Chaplin as "the little tramp," and as
the 1947 *Monsieur Verdoux*.

Making a Living, 1914. The little
tramp had not yet evolved.

tastic acrobatics—for example his somersault from a banister
down into a sofa with a lighted cigar in his mouth—are the only
palliating details.

8 Cruel, Cruel Love (1 reel)

FIRST NIGHT 26 March 1914
ALTERNATIVE TITLE Lord Helpus
MAIN FRENCH TITLE Charlot Marquis
DIRECTOR Mack Sennett
ACTORS Chaplin (Lord Helpus), Minta Durfee (his love),
Chester Conklin, Alice Davenport

A Chaplin film whose content is distinctly advanced. Here he plays
the rich lord whose love for an elegant young lady meets with
response. But their amorous moments are witnessed by a peeping

maid, who afterwards attacks the innocent lord in the park and embraces him. Alas, his chosen one happens to see the intermezzo from her veranda and breaks off the relationship. Beside himself with grief his lordship goes home and decides to commit suicide. Unbeknown to him, his servant swaps the dose of poison for a glass of water. His lordship takes a gulp, thinks he is dying and sees himself in hell among the devils, whereupon he 'plays the devil' himself.

A letter arrives, in which his beloved says the mistake has been cleared up—she still loves him! Simultaneously happy and in despair, his lordship rings for a doctor who hurries round with the ambulance. The young lady, who is half out of her wits after hearing about the tragedy, rushes in thinking she is coming to a deathbed.

His lordship undergoes violent treatment and the whole gang are finally thrown out. The truth is out and happiness is restored. Characteristic of this film, one of Chaplin's rarest, are the 'dream images' and Chaplin's wildly exaggerated mimicry.

During the filming of *Kid Auto Races at Venice*, 1914.

9 The Star Boarder (1 reel)

FIRST NIGHT 4 April 1914
ALTERNATIVE TITLES The Hash-House Hero, Landlady's Pet,
In Love with his Landlady
MAIN FRENCH TITLE Charlot Aime la Patronne
DIRECTOR Mack Sennett
ACTORS Chaplin (lodger), Minta Durfee (landlady),
Edgar Kennedy (landlord), Gordon Griffith (their son),
Alice Davenport (landlady's woman friend)

Chaplin, lodging in a boarding house, finds himself the favourite
of the pretty young landlady. All the other guests are jealous of
him. He takes liberties, pinches an extra bottle of beer from the
kitchen and goes for a walk with the landlady, with terrible consequences. After she has fallen off a ladder when picking apples and
is being cared for by Charlie, her little urchin of a son photographs
the couple in what appears to be a tender situation. Fortunately,
the boy goes on with his photographic studies and also snaps his
heavy father in a tête-à-tête with a riper beauty. In the evening the
boy arranges a slide show for the guests—a most painful situation
for all parties. It ends with a battle royal between the master of the
house and Chaplin. The latter wins, giving the enterprising scandal
photographer a good hiding.

10 Mabel at the Wheel (2 reel)

FIRST NIGHT 18 March 1914
ALTERNATIVE TITLES His Daredevil Queen, Hot Finish
MAIN FRENCH TITLE Mabel au Volant
DIRECTORS Mack Sennett and Mabel Normand
ACTORS Chaplin (jealous admirer), Mabel Normand
(sporting type), Chester Conklin (Mabel's daddy), Harry
McCoy (racing driver and Mabel's boy-friend), Mack Sennett
(reporter), Fred Mace, Joe Bordeaux (two suspect figures)

One of Chaplin's more noteworthy films, partly because it was his
first two-reeler, partly because of the controversy over its direction
which arose between Mabel Normand (whom Mack Sennett had
entrusted it to) and Chaplin, who had ideas of his own. These did
not agree with those of the self-assured—but intelligent and more
experienced—Mabel Normand. Chaplin even went so far as to

threaten to quit both Keystone and films altogether. In the end Mack Sennett had to intervene and direct it himself, but to some extent he respected Chaplin's views.

Mabel at the Wheel is a tough story about sabotage on the race track. Chaplin has abandoned his new-found costume; instead he appears in a black dress coat and a top hat. On his motorbike he tries to compete with his rival Harry's racing car, offers Mabel a trip on the pillion but drops her in a puddle, which naturally puts him out of court. In revenge he joins up with a couple of shady characters and abducts his rival just as the great race for the Vanderbilt Cup is about to start.

Harry is locked up in a shed. Mabel takes his place with a co-driver, and Chaplin does everything he can to sabotage the race. Among other things, he and his chums pour water on a curve causing the racing cars to skid hither and thither. Mabel's car overturns, but she escapes, resumes the race and wins it. Mack Sennett himself appears as an odd press representative, who finally arranges for the photographs to be taken of the victors. One of Chaplin's 'lowest', most unpleasant films.

11 Twenty Minutes of Love (1 reel)

FIRST NIGHT 20 April 1914
ALTERNATIVE TITLES He Loved Her So, Cops and Watches,
Love-Friend
MAIN FRENCH TITLE Charlot et le Chronomètre
DIRECTOR Mack Sennett
SCRIPTWRITER (presumably) Charlie Chaplin
ACTORS Chaplin (vagabond),
Edgar Kennedy (amorous young man on a bench),
Minta Durfee (his lady love),
Emma Clifton (another beauty),
Hank Mann (the sleeper),
Gordon Griffith (boy),
Joseph Swickard (old man who has had his pocket picked),
Chester Conklin (thief who steals watches).
About this last, there are certain reservations.
The action is not unlike Conklin's but the actor's slim figure
gives rise to some doubts.

Twenty Minutes of Love is the first in a long row of 'park' films shot in Westlake Park outside Los Angeles, whose lake, without any question, holds the world record for the numbers of policemen who have been pushed into it.

Charlie, a romantic type, is strolling in the park and finds himself alone among a number of loving couples. He parodies one couple on a bench by embracing a tree only to join in the game himself. In vain he tries to oust the man from the bench in order to flirt with his girl. On another bench another girl is asking her lover to give her a love token; he filches a pocket watch from a sleeping visitor, but on falling in with Charlie is, unawares, relieved of it. Charlie in his turn presents it to the girl, who abandons her former admirer.

Afterwards the watch is handed back to Charlie, who tries to sell it back to its original owner, who promptly summons a policeman. In the ensuing hullaballoo the large number of visitors to the park get pushed into the lake before Charlie, the victor, disappears with the girl.

12   Caught in a Cabaret (2 reel)

FIRST NIGHT 27 April 1914
ALTERNATIVE TITLES The Waiter, Jazz Waiter, Faking with Society
MAIN FRENCH TITLE Charlot Garçon de Café
DIRECTORS Mabel Normand and Charlie Chaplin
ACTORS Chaplin (waiter in a café), Mabel Normand (rich young society girl), Alice Davenport (her mother), Hank Mann (her father), Harry McCoy (Mabel's admirer),
Chester Conklin (waiter in the café), Mack Swain (proprietor), Edgar Kennedy (policeman), Minta Durfee (dancing waitress), Gordon Griffith (boy), Wallace MacDonald, Joseph Swickard, Phyllis Allen, Alice Howell, Leo White (personnel and customers)

The honour of having made this two-reeler must be divided between Chaplin and Mabel Normand, although it was scripted by Chaplin. Mabel plays a society girl, who is refusing to marry a supine count (Harry McCoy). Charlie has a job as waiter in a café in town. He is given an hour off, and during his promenade encounters Mabel and has a chance to rescue her from a thug who has scared away her admirer. Grateful, the girl introduces Charlie to her home, where, using a false visiting card, he presents himself as the Greek Ambassador. This definitely puts paid to the count.

Before the highly respected guest has to rush back to his duties as a waiter, the girl's parents invite him to their forthcoming garden party. The count, jealous, has trailed Charlie and discovered his destination. Charlie has to be chucker-out and knocks a troublesome customer over the head.

Dressed to kill, Charlie is a great success at the party. He manages to dupe everyone and charm Mabel. But once again he has to leave in haste, pleading 'pressure of business'. Seeing his chance, the rejected rival invites all the garden party guests to come with him to the café. The imposter is exposed, a scene culminating in a general uproar during which everyone, including Mabel, ends up on the floor. She quits Charlie, who is heart-broken.

13   Caught in the Rain (1 reel)

FIRST NIGHT 4 May 1914
ALTERNATIVE TITLES Who Got Stung?, At It Again,
In the Park (spurious title)
MAIN FRENCH TITLE Un Béguin de Charlot
DIRECTOR AND SCRIPTWRITER Charlie Chaplin
ACTORS Chaplin (a womaniser), Alice Davenport (the lady),
Mack Swain (her husband), Alice Howell

In this film, his thirteenth, Chaplin makes his début as a director. It is also scripted by him. *Caught in the Rain* is one of his many comedies which takes place in a hotel with park scenes. It should be noted that among its spurious titles when re-released in the USA and Europe the film has been misleadingly known as *In the Park*. The title has led to confusion among Chaplin collectors, since it really belongs to an Essanay film from 1915.

Caught in the Rain, too, was initially banned in Sweden, where its 'intimate' bedroom scenes were regarded as shocking. Otherwise one must credit it with some funny gags, which Chaplin polished up in his later films.

A married couple become separated in the park. Immediately Charlie appears and offers his company to the lady. The husband returns, flies into a rage and gives Charlie a drubbing. Charlie follows them back to their hotel where he books himself a room. The film's funniest scene is the one where Chaplin tries to force his way up the grand staircase from the foyer, a speciality he afterwards repeated in a number of films.

During the night the wife sleepwalks into Charlie's room. Her husband, who has been out for a walk, gets caught in a downpour and has to come back to the hotel. Finding the bedroom empty he looks for his wife. Charlie, terrified, conducts her back to her room, but when the husband appears has to climb out on to the window-sill in his pyjamas in the pouring rain. Police are summoned and he has to beat a retreat to his own bedroom. The police invade the hotel but in their turn are put to flight by Charlie, who finally tumbles into bed with the lady, while her husband, utterly exhausted by all he has been through, collapses in his own—a bed-time story, anno 1914.

14   A Busy Day (split reel)

FIRST NIGHT 7 June 1914
ALTERNATIVE TITLES Lady Charlie,
Militant Suffragette
MAIN FRENCH TITLE Madame Charlot
DIRECTOR Charlie Chaplin
ACTORS Chaplin (a jealous wife),
Mack Swain (Charlie's husband),
Alice Davenport [?] (the other woman)

For a long time very little was known about this film. For decades it was lost. Only its stills were extant. But in 1970 a copy appeared in the reduction print market in the USA. It was a happy discovery, for this is the first film in which Chaplin plays a female part: a real termagant. She becomes livid with rage when she discovers that her husband seems to be interested in another woman. The company appear at a military parade in a harbour town (the film was shot in the port of San Pedro) and after the husband has left 'lady Charlie' she keeps on getting in the way of a cameraman and film director—a direct copy of the scenes in *Kid Auto Races at Venice*. She kicks over the director, knocks down a policeman, and gets herself flung out among the crowd of spectators. Then, finding her husband and his new girl-friend listening to a military band, she assaults them and then turns on the police when they again try to intervene. In the end the husband takes action and pushes his vitriolic wife over the edge of the dock.

To judge from the final shot, she perishes in the waves. There are lively shots of shipping in the harbour. It has not been possible to say with certainty who plays the part of the wife's rival; but there is much to suggest it must be Alice Davenport.

15   The Fatal Mallet (1 reel)

FIRST NIGHT 1 June 1914
ALTERNATIVE TITLES The Pile Driver, The Rival Suitors,
Hit Him Again
MAIN FRENCH TITLE Le Maillot de Charlot
DIRECTORS Charlie Chaplin [probably], Mabel Normand
and Mack Sennett
ACTORS Chaplin, Mabel Normand, Mack Sennett and
Mack Swain

Charlie enters and disturbs Mabel's and Mack Sennett's tête-à-tête.
On a park swing he waits to see what will happen, throws a brick
at Mabel and gets it thrown back at him. Sennett and Charlie get
into a fight. Then the third aspirant to Mabel's favours (the slow-
witted Mack Swain) appears, and Mabel at once leaves the other
two for him. After a vain attempt to suppress their new rival, both
Charlie and Sennett flee to a barn, where Charlie finds a wooden
mallet, with which he clubs first Sennett and then Swain, locks
them both up in the barn and, victorious, gives Mabel a kick,
which instantly wins her heart. The film is a typical example of
the tough humour in Chaplin's 1914 films.

16   Her Friend the Bandit (1 reel)

FIRST NIGHT 4 June 1914
ALTERNATIVE TITLES Mabel's Flirtation, A Thief Catcher
MAIN FRENCH TITLE Le Flirt de Mabel

Her Friend the Bandit is the only Chaplin film of which hitherto
—(Jan 1973)—not a single copy of any kind has been traced. But
so many other films which have 'vanished for ever' have come to
light, that one can only suspect and hope that one day this one, too,
will be found.

Chaplin plays an elegant scoundrel who pays court to Mabel and
comes uninvited to a masquerade in the latter's home. He declares
that he is the Count de Beans, after the real count has been got out
of the way. But the false count makes such a fool of himself at the
party that the guests are shaken and Mabel summons the police,
which means a quick exit for the intruder. The film is a prototype
of later farces with the same theme, notably *The Count* and *The
Adventurer*.

Chaplin's supporting players. Numbers in parentheses indicate films in which each player appeared.

Phyllis Allen (13)
Billy Armstrong (11)
Lloyd Bacon (11)

Fatty Arbuckle (16)
Cecile Arnold (7)
Henry Bergman (20)

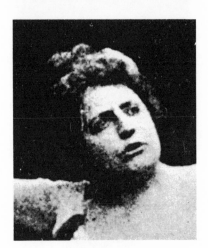

Eric Campbell (11)   Charlie Chase (8)
Chester Conklin (17)   Alice Davenport (9)
Minta Durfee (11)   Edgar Kennedy (10)   43

Hank Mann (9)
Mabel Normand (11)
Wesley Ruggles (8)

Harry McCoy (11)
Edna Purviance (35)
Mack Sennett (4)

Al St. John (7)
Mack Swain (17)
Leo White (21)

Slim Summerville (6)
Ben Turpin (4)
Tom Wilson (6)

45

17 The Knockout (2 reel)

FIRST NIGHT 11 June 1914
ALTERNATIVE TITLES Counted Out, The Pugilist
MAIN FRENCH TITLE Charlot et Fatty dans le Ring
DIRECTOR Mack Sennett
ACTORS Chaplin (referee), Fatty Arbuckle (challenger),
Edgar Kennedy (champion), Minta Durfee (Fatty's lady
friend), Hank Mann (boxer), Mack Swain (aggressive
gentleman in the box), Slim Summerville, Charlie Chase,
Al St John, Mack Sennett, Joe Bordeaux, Edward Cline,
Alice Howell (spectators), The Keystone Cops

This is really a Fatty film. Chaplin only appears as the referee in a
brief boxing sequence.

Fatty gets into difficulties with a gang of aggressive antagonists,
but gets his girl; to show how brave he is he challenges a champion
boxer to a match. During the match the bets go higher and higher.
Chaplin makes a famous contribution as a third man in the ring,
symbolising in a piece of pure ballet the panic-stricken little fellow
caught between two giants. After the match, Fatty flies into a
frenzy of rage and begins firing a pistol at random. The typical
wild Mack Sennett chase sequence over hill and dale and even the
roofs of houses provides the film with its almost surrealistic finale.

18 Mabel's Busy Day (1 reel)

FIRST NIGHT 13 June 1914
ALTERNATIVE TITLES Charlie and the Sausages, Love and
Lunch, Hot Dogs
MAIN FRENCH TITLE Charlot et les Saucisses
DIRECTORS Charlie Chaplin and Mabel Normand
ACTORS Chaplin (a flâneur), Mabel Normand (hot dog girl),
Edgar Kennedy (policeman), Chester Conklin (another
policeman), Slim Summerville,
Al St John, Charlie Chase,
Harry McCoy, Billie Bennett, Wallace MacDonald

The hot-dog girl, Mabel, offers the policeman, Chester, a sausage.
By way of a thank-you, she is allowed free into a race track. After
a brush with the law she is followed by Charlie, an elegant flâneur
with a flower in his buttonhole. Mabel's hot-dog stand is not doing

much business. People pinch her sausages, or else she has no change. Inside the race track Charlie continues to get into trouble with the police, pinching first a handkerchief from a lady among the spectators and then a hot dog from Mabel. She chases him, but Charlie gets away and pretends to be selling Mabel's sausages, which he sells off without anyone paying for them. Mabel discovers the sinner, summons the policeman Chester, and a new battle of fisticuffs takes place before Charlie manages to console the despairing Mabel. Apparently reconciled, he goes off with her.

The film contains a number of rowdy action shots on the race track. Chaplin deploys his whole register of kicks and swipes, and Mabel Normand her own abilities in the same line—hardly inferior to his.

19 Mabel's Married Life (1 reel)

FIRST NIGHT 20 June 1914
ALTERNATIVE TITLES When You're Married, The Squarehead
MAIN FRENCH TITLE Charlot et Mabel en Ménage
DIRECTORS Charlie Chaplin and Mabel Normand
ACTORS Chaplin (the husband), Mabel Normand (his wife),
Mack Swain (Mr Wellington, an enterprising sportsman),
Alice Howell (Mack Swain's wife), Charlie Murray, Harry
McCoy, Wallace MacDonald (bar customers)

Chaplin appears in a top hat and frock coat. He and Mabel are taking their leisure in the park when they are accosted by Mack Swain, a lady-killer, who impudently begins courting Mabel. Charlie does not dare to intervene effectively. Not until Mr Wellington's infuriated wife turns up is the matter solved. Charlie goes off to console himself in a bar, while Mabel, embittered at her ineffectual husband, goes off alone.

Seeing a full-size boxer's dummy outside a shop she orders it to be sent to her home. Her hope is that Charlie will go into training and wipe out the insult. A funny and unique scene in which Mabel, in her room, mimics to perfection Charlie's way of walking.

Charlie, drunker and drunker, is being bullied by the other drinkers, including Mr Wellington. He comes home to find another man—the dummy—in his room, takes it for Mr Wellington and goes to the attack, an exceedingly funny sequence in which the dummy one moment knocks down Charlie and the next Mabel, after Charlie has first tried to make the intruder see reason.

20 Laughing Gas (1 reel)

FIRST NIGHT 9 July 1914
ALTERNATIVE TITLES Tuning his Ivories, The Dentist,
Down and Out, Busy Little Dentist
MAIN FRENCH TITLE Charlot Dentiste
DIRECTOR AND SCRIPTWRITER Charlie Chaplin
ACTORS Chaplin (dentist's assistant), Fritz Schade (Dr Pain,
the dentist), Alice Howell (his wife), Mack Swain, Joseph
Swickard and Slim Summerville (patients) Joseph Suther-
land [?] (second dentist's assistant)

Laughing Gas is the first of the series of films, only once interrupted, in which Chaplin is both director and script-writer. Charlie
begins his day's work by pretending to be the dentist, but soon
gives away his real status by placing the spittoons on the kitchen
table where his colleague is just having breakfast.

The dentist arrives and has trouble with his first patient (Joseph
Swickard), who cannot stand the anaesthetic gas. He wakes up in
paroxysms of laughter, but Charlie intervenes and knocks him out
with a club and puts him to sleep again.

The dentist, troubled, sends his assistant to a drug store to buy
some medicine. There Charlie falls in with Mack Swain. In the
course of a dispute on the street the latter gets a brick in his face
and has to join the dentist's patients.

Also mixed up in the scuffle is the dentist's good-looking young
wife, who has been taking a walk. Charlie happens to pull her skirt
off. In a shocked state she goes home and rings up her husband.
Now Charlie has the dentist's reception to himself, he seizes his
chance for an intimate tête-à-tête with a pretty patient in the
dentist's chair and with a gigantic pair of pincers pulls out the
wrong tooth from another patient. When Mack Swain arrives and
recognises the cause of the trouble in the street, a furious fight
breaks out. Everyone, including the dentist, who has come back,
and his wife, is involved.

21 The Property Man (2 reel)

FIRST NIGHT 1 Aug 1914
ALTERNATIVE TITLES Getting his Goat, The Rustabout,
Vamping Venus
MAIN FRENCH TITLE Charlot Garçon de Théatre

DIRECTOR AND SCRIPTWRITER Charlie Chaplin
ACTORS Chaplin (production manager and factotum in a small
vaudeville theatre), Fritz Schade (athlete), Phyllis Allen,
Norma Nichols and Alice Davenport (vaudeville artistes),
Mack Sennett (member of the audience in a pullover),
Joe Bordeaux (old actor), Charles Bennett, Harry McCoy,
Lee Morris

This film represents a small step forward in Chaplin's development. However, although he succeeds in distilling the essence of
burlesque, his humour is still of the tough type—for example,
when Charlie kicks an older assistant in the face as he lies on the
ground and lets him be crushed under a trunk. That an assistant
producer's life is no bed of roses is made plain in the film's first
half, in which Charlie has problems with the actors' baggage and
their rival claims to the star's dressing room. The film is full of
misadventures, which culminate during the performance in an
orgy of scene changes, wrong entries and finally a scene with a fireman's hose, all precursors of similar scenes in *A Night in the
Show* and *A King in New York*. Charlie is at his funniest when
he exposes the athlete by juggling with his bogus weights.

22 The Face on the Bar Room Floor (1 reel)

FIRST NIGHT 10 Aug 1914
ALTERNATIVE TITLES The Ham Artist, The Ham Actor
MAIN FRENCH TITLE Charlot Peintre
DIRECTOR Charlie Chaplin
ACTORS Chaplin (an artist on the downgrade), Cecile Arnold
(Madeleine, his beloved), Fritz Schade (her new love),
Vivian Edwards (model), Chester Conklin, Hank Mann,
Harry McCoy, Wallace MacDonald (habitués)

An unusual Chaplin film, a satire based on the poem *The Face on
the Bar Room Floor,* by Hugh Antoine d'Arcy, with a genuine
Chaplinesque vignette, not drawn from the poem, to round it off.
Remarkably enough, the theme is precisely the same as that of
Maurice Chevalier's famous song 'Valentine'—a young man who
is in love with 'the world's most beautiful woman', but who is
abandoned by her. Later he meets up with her; but now she has
a husband and a child. Seeing how gross her figure has become
and how her beauty has faded he thanks his lucky stars he has
escaped so cruel a fate.

The entire poem is quoted in the script. To it Charlie adds a visual depiction of how the artist, in utter despair, experiences his life tragedy in a bar. He is a well-known painter, who courts Madeleine; but a wealthy client who has been sitting for his portrait wins Madeleine's favours. Whereupon the artist in a fit of rage destroys his client's portrait and tries to draw a picture of his beloved on the bar room floor, but gets chucked out.

Some years later he meets her in a park together with her husband and a horde of children. Though she does not recognise him, her husband does. Finally Charlie makes the first of his famous exits in which he shakes off his troubles and 'goes on life's way'. The theme recurs several times afterwards in Chaplin's production for example, in *The Tramp, The Circus* and *Modern Times*.

The farewell scene's proper position in the film is a matter of opinion. Several Chaplin experts place it in the middle, Chaplin's collapse in the bar, they think, should be the finale—like the hero of the poem he is giving up worldly things. Perhaps they are right. Personally I am certain that Chaplin wanted his 'customary' blithe exit to come at the end. The film exists in both versions.

23   Recreation (split reel)

FIRST NIGHT 13 Aug 1944
ALTERNATIVE TITLE Spring Fever
MAIN FRENCH TITLE Fièvre Printanière
DIRECTOR AND SCRIPTWRITER Charlie Chaplin
ACTORS Charlie Chaplin (the idler in the park), Charlie Murray [?] (a seaman on a park bench), Norma Nichols (the girl). No credits have been preserved (as is also the case with *A Busy Day* and many other early Chaplin films), but the seaman resembles Murray and he has been ascribed the part. The policeman has not been identified.

This is a minor 'park story' film, whose charm lies in the almost ballet-like formal rhythm of Charlie's controversies with the seaman and the policeman.

Charlie, love-sick as usual, is walking in the park. A girl has just left a seaman asleep on a bench, and joins Charlie on another. In vain Charlie tries to introduce himself. The seaman wakes up, sees them sitting there together and goes to the attack. Charlie flees but gets involved in a virtuosic brick-throwing act with his rival, who replies in kind. A policeman appears, only to be immediately struck by a flying brick as is a colleague who also tries to intervene. Charlie and the seaman are arrested, a fight breaks out on the quay and both policeman and the seaman end up in 'the drink' where they are joined by Charlie and the girl. In its composition the film is so extremely like the earlier *Twenty Minutes of Love* (first night 20 April 1914) that one may almost suspect it of using up a certain amount of leftover material from the earlier film, to which new takes have been added. Claims that Mabel Normand, Mack Swain, Chester Conklin and Alice Davenport have roles in *Recreation* are incorrect.

24 The Masquerader (1 reel)

FIRST NIGHT 27 Aug 1914
ALTERNATIVE TITLES Putting One Over, The Female
Impersonator, His New Profession (unauthentic title)
MAIN FRENCH TITLE Charlot Grande Coquette
DIRECTOR Charlie Chaplin
ACTORS Chaplin (film extra and film star in disguise),
Fatty Arbuckle (film actor), Chester Conklin, (ditto),
Fritz Schade (ditto), Charlie Murray (the film
director),
Charlie Chase, Harry McCoy, Cecile Arnold (fair),
Vivian Edwards (dark)

Once again Charlie is in a film studio, this time as an actor. He shares a dressing-table with Fatty Arbuckle and first appears without a moustache: then, donning his familiar garb, he plays out a dramatic scene in front of the camera, but because he is busy flirting with two pretty actresses misses his own entrance cue. After he has ruined the drama, in which a child is to be saved from a murderer's knife (Fritz Schade), Chester Conklin gets his chance; but Charlie again intervenes and he makes a mess of it. Charlie is kicked out of the studios.

When he comes back he is dressed up as a beautiful lady. Her charms instantly captivate the director, who gives Lady Charlie the dressing room to herself and makes amorous approaches. But Charlie reveals himself for what he is; and Lady Charlie never gets her part in films. Again there is an uproar and Charlie's final flight ends at the bottom of a well, an end to his career which the bystanders, reverent in the presence of death, salute by solemnly removing their hats. A finale in which Chaplin found the script too much for him.

The best features of this film are Chaplin's immaculate female impersonation and the interiors from the film studio.

25 His New Profession (1 reel)

FIRST NIGHT 31 Aug 1914
ALTERNATIVE TITLES The Good for Nothing, Helping Himself
MAIN FRENCH TITLE Charlot Garde-Malade
DIRECTOR AND SCRIPTWRITER Charlie Chaplin
ACTORS Chaplin (amateur male nurse), Fritz Schade (old gentleman), Charley Chase (young man), Norma Nichols (his lady love), Harry McCoy (policeman) Cecile Arnold (another girl)

We see Charlie sitting on a bench, reading *The Police Gazette*—an introductory scene which has been erroneously ascribed to *Recreation*. He snips out a bit of the newspaper, perhaps because he sees he is 'wanted', though this is not quite clear.

Later he meets up with a young couple in love. The man, who has to look after his crippled and querulous old uncle in a wheel-chair, promises Charlie a dollar if he will take over the job: a thankless task, as Charlie soon discovers. For their part, the young couple begin to quarrel; and when the young man next turns up it is with a new dollie (Cecile Arnold), who chances to drop a bag of eggs on the path in the park. Charlie, of course, slips up on the eggs and goes flying while trying to manoeuvre the wheel-chair.

Now he places it out on the jetty, close to another man also in a wheel-chair to which a notice 'Invalid' is affixed, together with a beggar's tin. Charlie switches these objects to the old man he is supposed to be taking care of, and before long there are profits from a generous passer-by. Charlie goes into a bar where he uses the alms to buy himself a much-needed glass of liquor; after which, feeling merry, he returns to the jetty, there to become simultaneously involved in a tête-à-tête with the young man's abandoned lady love and in a controversy with the uncle, whose crippled leg is subjected to the same rough treatment as three years later Eric Campbell's was to be in *The Cure*.

Finally Charlie pushes wheel-chair and occupant over the brink of the jetty, settles accounts with the beggar—who turns out to have been a charlatan—and likewise with the young man who, wild with jealousy, has now returned. He also tackles two policemen who put in an appearance, one of whom ends up in the water. The film ends with the other policeman unjustly arresting the uncle for causing a public disturbance, while Charlie beats up his rival and takes the girl. Funny in its way, the film contains some disagreeably sadistic humour.

26 The Rounders (1 reel)

FIRST NIGHT 7 Sept 1914
ALTERNATIVE TITLES Revelry, Two of a Kind,
Oh, What a Night!, The Love Thief, Tip, Tap, Toe
MAIN FRENCH TITLE Charlot et Fatty en Bombe
DIRECTOR AND SCRIPTWRITER Charlie Chaplin
ACTORS Chaplin (husband on the loose), Fatty Arbuckle
(second husband on the loose), Phyllis Allen (Charlie's wife),
Minta Durfee (Fatty's wife—as she was in reality),
Fritz Schade (elderly restaurant habitué, who has seen
better days), Charlie Chase, Al St John, Wallace MacDonald
(restaurant personnel)

This is the only film in which Chaplin, oddly enough, was accused by the censorship of imitating himself. The first certificate issued by the Swedish censors, not only totally banned the film but also declared that Chaplin's role was played by Billie Ritchie.

The subject? One is tempted to frighten the reader with this drastic description from 27 August 1915:

> Two drunken gentlemen are living in the same hotel. One of them is beaten up by his wife, the other mishandles his own. First the two men get into a fight, but avail themselves of a moment when their wives have got into a dispute to grab their money and set out on a new round of drunkenness. Their inebriation becomes steadily greater. The two men, who by now are become 'perfect beasts', drop off to sleep in a restaurant, where they have made themselves up beds with the tablecloths etc, but are driven out and find a refuge in a rowing boat, in which they again drop off to sleep. The boat fills with water, and as far as one can see both drunks get drowned.

That was the Swedish verdict in 1914, and it is correct as far as it goes. Possibly one may surmise that the couple of inebriates voluntarily sought death to escape a worse fate—life with their moralistic shrews of wives. This was the third time Chaplin had allowed himself to die on the screen.

27 The New Janitor (1 reel)

FIRST NIGHT 24 Sept 1914
ALTERNATIVE TITLES The Porter, The Blundering Boob,
The New Porter
MAIN FRENCH TITLE Charlot Portier
DIRECTOR AND SCRIPTWRITER Charlie Chaplin
ACTORS Chaplin (janitor), Fritz Schade (his boss),
Minta Durfee (the secretary), Jack Dillon (the thief),
Al St John

In a way this is a preliminary study for *The Bank*, made in the
following year. The office manager of a firm where Charlie has a
job as janitor receives a blackmail letter from a gambler, Luke
Connor, demanding that he shall immediately pay up his gambling
debts, or else.

At that moment Charlie happens to chuck a bucket of water
out of the window, soaking his boss on the street, and is instantly
sacked. The office closes and the boss breaks into the safe in order
to get the cash he so desperately needs. Surprised by his secretary,
he attacks her but she has time to ring the bell for the janitor.
Charlie, just about to leave the building, returns and tangles with
the thief. Grabbing his revolver he saves both girl and money.
After a misunderstanding when the police arrive (naturally they
take Charlie for the thief) the hero is rewarded and reinstated in
his job.

This is the first Chaplin film with a trace of sentimentality to it,
when Charlie is fired and 'martyrised', before making his comeback as victor.

28 Those Love Pangs (1 reel)

FIRST NIGHT 10 Oct 1914
ALTERNATIVE TITLES The Rival Mashers, Busted Hearts
MAIN FRENCH TITLE Charlot Rival d'Amour
DIRECTOR AND SCRIPTWRITER Charlie Chaplin
ACTORS Chaplin (solitary and love-sick), Chester Conklin
(lady-killer), Norma Nichols (landlady), Cecile Arnold and
Vivian Edwards (two pretty dollies in the park),
Edgar Kennedy (their gentleman friend)

The theme is the same as in *Twenty Minutes of Love*. Charlie and Chester, rivals for the favours of their lovely landlady, stick forks into each other in their efforts to meet her in private. After which both go out into the park, where Chester meets and wins the heart of a girl (Cecile Arnold), while Charlie falls for another (Vivian Edwards), who unfortunately has a stupid gentleman friend in attendance.

Jilted, Charlie contemplates suicide but is prevented by a policeman from jumping into the lake. Later he settles accounts with the tall gentleman friend, whom he pulls into the lake with the aid of his walking stick. The girls, terrified by the row, leave the park and seek romance in a cinema. But there, too, Charlie turns up. Again he flirts with them, this time in the stalls; but Chester and his chum come into the cinema, where they contrive to change places with the girls without Charlie noticing it, after which they flings themselves upon him. After an uproar in which the entire audience is involved, Charlie is chucked out through the screen.

29   Dough and Dynamite (2 reel)

FIRST NIGHT 26 Aug 1914
ALTERNATIVE TITLES The Doughnut Designer, The Cook,
The New Cook
MAIN FRENCH TITLE Charlot Mitron
DIRECTOR Charlie Chaplin
SCRIPTWRITER Mack Sennett
ACTORS Chaplin (waiter and baker), Chester Conklin
(ditto), Fritz Schade (owner of the restaurant), Phyllis Allen
(guest), Charlie Chase, Slim Summerville, Wallace
MacDonald, Cecile Arnold (waitress), Vivian Edwards
(waitress), Norma Nichols (a client), Edgar Kennedy

Charlie and Chester are waiters in a French restaurant which bakes its own bread. Charlie, waiting at table, suffers various mishaps. One diner after another is driven away by his smiting them with pieces of tart. Suddenly the bakers start a 'wildcat' strike, Charlie and Chester have to put on their white coats and take over their jobs. In a fight with his mate, Charlie makes virtuosic use of the dough, showing off his prowess to the admiring waitresses. But now the strikers are hatching a terrible plot. They put dynamite in a piece of bread, and an unsuspecting little girl delivers it to the cake counter. After various mixups the bread finds its way into the bakery oven, where the dynamite explodes, causing havoc. In the last shot Charlie's face emerges from a heap of dough. A film in which Charlie's mime blends advantageously with Mack Sennett's gift for comic situations.

30 Gentlemen of Nerve (1 reel)

FIRST NIGHT 29 Oct 1914
ALTERNATIVE TITLES Some Nerve, Charlie at the Races
MAIN FRENCH TITLE Charlot et Mabel aux Courses
DIRECTOR AND SCRIPTWRITER Charlie Chaplin
ACTORS Chaplin (who has let himself into a motor race, free of charge), Mack Swain (ditto), Mabel Normand, Chester Conklin (Mabel's gentleman friend), Edgar Kennedy (policeman), Phyllis Allen, Slim Summerville

Chester invites Mabel to a speedway race. Charlie, too, turns up with Mack. As they are letting themselves in through a hole in the paling, Mack gets stuck. A policeman appears, but Charlie borrows a soda siphon from a member of the public and squirts the policeman until Mack can free himself. In the grandstand Mabel and Chester fall out, and she abandons her beau in favour of Charlie.

The row among the spectators goes on. Chester counterattacks and is beaten up by Charlie; falls into the hands of a policeman, who also seizes Mack, while Charlie and Mabel triumphantly witness their departure for gaol. There are a few shots of racing cars in this primitive burlesque farce, which is hardly worthy either of Charlie or his art.

31 His Musical Career (1 reel)

FIRST NIGHT 7 Nov 1914
ALTERNATIVE TITLES The Piano Movers, Musical Tramps
MAIN FRENCH TITLE Charlot Déménageur
DIRECTOR AND SCRIPTWRITER Charlie Chaplin
ACTORS Chaplin (employed by a removal firm), Mack Swain (ditto), Fritz Schade (Mr Rich), Alice Howell (Mrs Rich), Charlie Chase (manager of a music shop), Joe Bordeaux (artist), Norma Nichols (his daughter)

Charlie and Mack, employees of a removal firm, receive an order to deliver a piano to the wealthy Mr Rich, address 666 Prospect Hill, and at the same time to fetch back a piano from a seedy artist

Chaplin, with Mabel Normand and
Mack Swain, in *Gentleman of Nerve,*
1914.

who has been unable to keep up his hire purchase payments;
address 999 Prospect Hill. Naturally they confuse the addresses.

The journey with the mule-drawn cart is eventful, and in its
last stages an exact precursor of Laurel and Hardy's famous two-
reeler from 1932, *The Music Box.* Both contain precisely the same
gags. In the one case it is Mack Swain who, because of Charlie's
clumsiness, is crushed under the piano; in the other it is Hardy
who is placed in the same predicament by Laurel.

There is an exquisite scene in which Charlie, after carrying the
piano's entire weight, walks about like a dwarf. At the house of
Mr Rich only Mrs Rich and butler are in, and the removal men
carry out their task *con furore.* In the street they encounter the
indignant Mr Rich; the piano runs away down the hill, cannot
be stopped, and finally, together with Charlie and Mack, ends up
in a lake. Charlie manages to play a few final chords before it sinks.

32 His Trysting Place (2 reel)

FIRST NIGHT 9 Nov 1914
ALTERNATIVE TITLES Family House, Family Home
MAIN FRENCH TITLE Charlot Papa

Charlie Chaplin
ACTORS Chaplin (paterfamilias), Mabel Normand (his wife),
Mack Swain (second husband), Phyllis Allen (his wife)

The film consists of two married couples in a comedy of errors with
a clearly defined action pattern. Charlie is married to the smash-
ing Mabel, who despairs of her inept husband, curses him when
he handles their baby carelessly and generally orders him about.
She tells him to go to a drugstore and buy a baby's bottle with
milk for the child.

Meanwhile a more loving scene is being played out in a lodging
house between Mack and his wife. In another room a girl is writing
a *billet doux* to her lover, asking him to meet her at the usual
place in the park. The girl asks Mack to post her letter for her,
and he stuffs it into his coat pocket.

Charlie, having carried out his errand, slips into a little restaurant, where Mack is sitting at the bar. The two of them eat an
extremely comic meal together, which ends with a dispute. When
they part company each takes the other's coat by mistake.

Charlie gets home. Mabel finds the love letter where the baby's
bottle should be, and flies into a rage. After his drubbing, Mack
has sought consolation with his wife on a park bench. Suddenly
he too finds himself in an awful predicament. His wife, finding
the bottle, imagines he has an illegitimate child.

Charlie is driven out of the house with an ironing board and
flees to the park, his wife at his heels. There he again runs into
trouble. Mabel and Mack are trying to console each other, and
for a while Mack has to take over the baby. His wife, seeing the
infant in his arms, faints. However, the mutual error with the
overcoats is discovered. Charlie hands over the fatal love letter to
Mack's wife and gets back his bottle. And the wretched Mack looks
forward to a trouncing.

33 Tillie's Punctured Romance (6 reel)

FIRST NIGHT 14 Nov 1914
ALTERNATIVE TITLES Tillie's Nightmare, For the Love of
Tillie, Marie's Millions, Tillie's Big Romance
MAIN FRENCH TITLE Le Roman Comique de Charlot et
de Lolotte
DIRECTOR Mack Sennett
SCRIPTWRITER Hampton Del Ruth, on the basis of

Edgar Smith's musical comedy *Tillie's Nightmare*
(music by Baldwin Sloane)
ACTORS Chaplin (a professional Don Juan, after women's
money), Marie Dressler (Tillie, the farmer's daughter),
Mack Swain (her father), Mabel Normand (Charlie's girl-
friend), Charles Bennett (Mr Banks the multi-millionaire,
Tillie's uncle), Charlie Chase and Charlie Murray
(policemen), Chester Conklin (Mr Whoozis, an old
friend of Mr Banks), Edgar Kennedy (the restaurant owner),
Gordon Griffith (newsboy), Minta Durfee, Phyllis Allen,
Billie Bennett, Alice Davenport, Harry McCoy, Alice
Howell, Joe Bordeaux, G. C. Ligon, Wallace MacDonald,
Slim Summerville, Hank Mann, Al St John, Eddie Sutherland
and members of the Keystone Cops

Chaplin, a professional seducer from the town, sets off for the
countryside in search of fresh fields. While playing with her dog a
chubby farmer's daughter (Tillie) happens to hit Charlie with a
brick. Overwhelmed with remorse she takes him to her father's
farm to recover. Charlie quickly realises the old fellow is quite
wealthy and seizes his chance. In a tête-à-tête on a fence he charms
Tillie with descriptions of the delights of the big city. Finally she
agrees to elope with him—and takes her father's money.

Now we are in town. Charlie, piloting Tillie through the traffic,
nearly gets run over. The couple are discovered by Charlie's girl-
friend Mabel who, passionately jealous, follows them into a restaurant. Here Tillie makes the heady acquaintance of alcohol. As
Tillie dances wildly with one partner after another, Mabel talks
Charlie into taking her well-lined handbag; and they vanish. After
a nasty dispute with the police, Tillie, tousled and disappointed,
ends up in clink. However, she contacts her rich uncle and is let
out. The uncle wishes to have nothing to do with her.

Charlie and Mabel go to a cinema, where they are much shaken
to see a film about the terrible fate of a thieving couple who have
made a similar coup. Hastily they leave the cinema, but cannot
help spending Tillie's money. One day they enter a restaurant
where the wretched Tillie has taken a job as a waitress. She recognises Charlie, throws a tray at him, and faints.

Charlie and Mabel retire to a bench in the park. Here Charlie
happens to read in the newspaper that Tillie's wealthy uncle has
died while climbing a mountain. He has left her three million
dollars. Jilting Mabel, he slips away, rushes off to the restaurant
and after a certain amount of discussion manages to get Tillie to

go with him to a clergyman. Hearing she has inherited a fortune, Tillie begins to realise why Charlie is in such a hurry to marry her, and reproaches him. But the pair are reconciled, and move into the millionaire uncle's villa. There, waited on by a large staff of servants, they start living it up. Mabel tracks them down. To keep an eye on her former fiancé she takes a job as housemaid.

At a big society event arranged by Charlie and Tillie, Tillie finds Charlie in a delicate situation with Mabel. She goes berserk. Finally she gets hold of a revolver and chases the guilty couple round the house. At that moment the uncle reappears. Reports of his death were unfounded.

The uncle drives the whole lot of them out of the house and summons the police. In a fantastic finale on a pier, all are chased by the police, who drive over the brink and end up in the water as do Charlie, Tillie and Mabel. But their lives are saved. The women make it up between them and agree that Charlie is a scoundrel not worthy of either of them. Submitting to his fate, he is taken away by the police.

This film was a milestone in the careers of three of its participants: Mack Sennett, Chaplin and Marie Dressler. In the summer of 1914 Sennett, who was a close friend of his former employer David W. Griffith, heard that Griffith was working on his long feature film *Birth of a Nation*. If Griffith can make a war drama in twelve reels, Sennett thought, then he could certainly make a farce lasting for six. So far he had never gone further than two.

Everyone in the studios, not to say Sennett's backers, regarded the project as insane—even though his star Charlie Chaplin, after thirty-two shorts, was already a big name in movies. But not even with Mabel Normand to play against him was Charlie's name enough for a long film. Sennett got the ambitious idea of signing up Marie Dressler, who at that time was riding high as a stage actress. A massive not to say explosive prima donna, she had just made a big hit in a stage comedy, *Tillie's Nightmare*. No one believed Sennett would bring it off, but he had known Marie Dressler for years and offered her a fee—staggering at that time— of $2,500 a week, or ten times what Chaplin was getting!

When Marie Dressler turned up in Hollywood in September 1914, a start had not even been made on the script. In despair Sennett shut the collaborators in a room (together with a battery of champagne bottles), and refused to let any of them out until they had produced a synopsis. Someone hit on the idea of basing the film's action on the play *Tillie's Nightmare*. The plot was worked out in a flash, as was indeed imperative; Marie Dressler was on the payroll from the day of her arrival in Hollywood.

Tillie's Punctured Romance was a smash hit, and because of its 'impossible' length, made a sensation. Not until well into the twenties did any other director dare to make a farce of equal length. It was also the beginning of Marie Dressler's career in movies—a career which culminated brilliantly in the Garbo film *Anna Christie*. For Chaplin, too, it was a major break-through.

A number of film historians who have not seen this film ascribe its success mostly to Marie Dressler and under-value Chaplin's contribution. This is wrong. Chaplin's role is as big and as rewarding as hers, and Mabel Normand also made a major contribution. It is significant that when the film had its première in Sweden Marie Dressler's name did not so much as appear in the publicity. It was a Chaplin film. All in all it took fourteen weeks to shoot.

34 Getting Acquainted (1 reel)

FIRST NIGHT 5 Dec 1914
ALTERNATIVE TITLES A Fair Exchange, Exchange is No Robbery, Hullo Everybody
MAIN FRENCH TITLE Charlot et Mabel en Promenade
DIRECTOR AND SCRIPTWRITER Charlie Chaplin
ACTORS Chaplin (Mr Sniffles), Phyllis Allen (his wife), Mabel Normand (flirtatious young wife), Mack Swain (her husband), Edgar Kennedy (policeman), Harry McCoy (Turk), Cecile Arnold (a girl)

A typical 'park film', in which two married couples swap partners. Charlie is taking a walk with his lawful spouse when he meets Mack and Mabel. Improper emotions develop, and a jealous game of hide-and-seek begins. A policeman who is looking for a professional Don Juan appears and joins in the game, as does, inexplicably, a Turk—one of those costumed characters who not uncommonly are introduced into Chaplin's short films. In the end Charlie is dragged away by his wife, out of reach of all amorous perils.

As a farce it is astonishingly primitive to have been made so late in the Keystone series.

35 His Prehistoric Past (2 reel)

FIRST NIGHT 7 Dec 1914
ALTERNATIVE TITLES A Dream, King Charlie, The Caveman
MAIN FRENCH TITLE Charlot Nudiste

An early Karno poster. Chaplin is at left, second from bottom. Stan Laurel is at bottom right.

Chaplin (center) with friends from the Fred Karno Music Hall Company in London, about 1906.

Shooting a film. Chaplin is instructing his favorite cameraman, Rollie Totheroth.

DIRECTOR AND SCRIPTWRITER Charlie Chaplin
ACTORS Chaplin (Mr Weakchin), Mack Swain (King Low-
Brow), Gene March (the king's favourite wife),
Fritz Schade (Ku-Ku the medicine man, friend of the king),
Al St John (one of the cavemen), Cecile Arnold (a
cavewoman)

This is the first film in which the action throughout is in the form
of a dream. He may have got the idea from a sketch, 'Jimmy the
Fearless', which he had played for Fred Karno, and in which
Jimmy too wakes up from a dream. Dream sequences occur later in
The Bank (1915), *Shoulder Arms* (1918), *Sunnyside* (1919), *The
Kid* (1921) and *The Idle Class* (1921), in all of which, as in *His
Prehistoric Past*, Charlie wakes up to a crude and unpleasant
reality.

Charlie, asleep on a bench in the park, dreams he is back in the
Stone Age—a theme which several other comedians, including
Buster Keaton, used. He is living in an island paradise, where King
Low-Brow rules over a whole harem of wives. Charlie appears clad
in skins, but not without his bowler hat. He learns how to use a
club, flirts with all the women and falls in love with the king's
favourite wife Sum-Babee. Ku-Ku, the king's medicine man, discovers them in a tête-à-tête and tries to intervene by putting an
arrow through Charlie, but the king reprimands him. The king's
friendship soon turns to jealousy and wrath, however, when he
hears that the stranger has been taking a swim with his beautiful
wife. Charlie wriggles out of the situation by explaining that she
was drowning—he has saved her life. Charlie is forgiven, but the
truce is brief. During a hunting trip a new quarrel breaks out on
the brink of a precipice, and the king is shoved over the edge.

Assuming that the king is done for, Charlie returns to the cave
folk and proclaims himself king. But Ku-Ku finds the real king,
who has got stuck in a cleft in the rock, and helps him out. They
surprise Charlie together with Sum-Babee. Charlie is hit on the
head by a heavy stone and knocked out—to wake up on a park
bench, where he is being shaken by a policeman.

The Essanay Period

On 2 January 1915 Charlie Chaplin left Mack Sennett for the Essanay Company, with a contracted salary of $1,250 a week, or about seven times as much as he had been getting when he had first started with Keystone. Sennett tried to keep him to the bitter end, but could not outbid the rival firm.

Chaplin's first film for Essanay was made in the company's studio in Chicago at 1333 Argyle Street; but then, because of the severe climate, they moved over to another Essanay studio at Niles near San Francisco. There five films were shot. Then the company moved again, this time to settle permanently at Majestic Studio on Fairview Avenue, Los Angeles.

No longer was it a question of shooting films at breakneck pace. Characteristic of Chaplin's Essanay films is a stronger accent on his personal style, more carefully designed sets and more thoroughly worked out scripts. Not that there was any question of a 'script', in the proper sense of the term. Charlie held most of it in his head. No film took less than a fortnight to shoot, and many took more.

Whether Chaplin can be said to have made fourteen or fifteen films for Essanay is a matter of interpretation. The fifteenth was not edited together until 1918, out of Chaplin material from films shot in 1915. (See chapter on Chaplin's 'spurious' films.)

It was during the Essanay period that Chaplin seriously began to develop the tramp character that was to reach maturity in the following year in his film for Mutual.

36 His New Job (2 reel)

FIRST NIGHT 1 Feb 1915
ALTERNATIVE TITLE Charlie's New Job
MAIN FRENCH TITLE Charlot Débute
DIRECTOR AND SCRIPTWRITER Charlie Chaplin
ACTORS Chaplin (a film extra),

Frank J. Coleman (assistant director),
Ben Turpin (his assistant),
Charlotte Mineau (star),
Charles Insley (director),
Leo White (actor, the little hussar officer),
Bud Jamison (the star who turns up late),
Billy Armstrong, Agnes Ayres and
Gloria Swanson (extras)
The cameraman was Rollie Totheroh. From now on—
towards the end with assistants—Totheroh was to be
responsible for the camera work of all Chaplin films
up to *Monsieur Verdoux*.

It is surprising to find the name of Gloria Swanson, afterwards so
celebrated, among the extras. She served her apprenticeship with
Mack Sennett (though she long denied the fact) and appeared in a
number of his films as a bathing beauty. But this is her sole Chaplin film. Another future star was Agnes Ayres who six years later
was to play the female lead against Rudolph Valentino in *The
Sheik*.

Charlie is looking for a job in a film studio. After out-manoeuvr-
ing his rival, Ben Turpin, he approaches the producer. He is given
a role as an extra but gets lost in the studio where the shooting is
just going on, causes chaos, and is sent off and told to assist the
carpenter. Even in this job he is impossible. When one of the chief
actors in the film fails to turn up, however, the director gives
Charlie his chance, and his job helping the carpenter is given to
Ben Turpin. Actually a game of dice is more to Charlie's taste than
film-acting. But when in the end he is thrown into the film's action,
chaos again ensues. Charlie makes a mess of his scene, knocks over
a pillar and pays such vigorous court to the primadonna that she
loses her skirt. The whole thing ends with a general bout of fisticuffs, in which the male star—who has now turned up—joins in.
Charlie comes out victor.

37   A Night Out (2 reel)

FIRST NIGHT 15 Feb 1915
ALTERNATIVE TITLES Champagne Charlie,
Charlie's Drunken Daze
MAIN FRENCH TITLE Charlot Fait la Noce
DIRECTOR AND SCRIPTWRITER Charlie Chaplin
ACTORS Chaplin (a night jay), Ben Turpin (his chum),

Bud Jamison (the head waiter), Edna Purviance (his wife),
Leo White (a 'French' customer in the restaurant),
Fred Goodwins

This was the first film in which Edna Purviance was Chaplin's leading lady. She was to play in thirty-four more of his films.

Charlie and Ben have set out early on a pub-crawl. When we meet them on their way to a restaurant they are already both dead-drunk; and so remain throughout the film. It is a repetition of Charlie's and Fatty's behaviour in *The Rounders,* but here the acting has been worked out in greater detail. The diner who comes off worst is the 'Frenchman' (Leo White).

Finally he summons the head waiter. The latter's attempts to deal with the irrepressible Ben are incredibly funny. Finally Ben is chucked out. Chaplin meanwhile has time to insult Leo's new lady friend, flings a pie at her furious partner, and thereafter spruces himself up in the fountain before his own fate is settled, and he too ends up outside on the pavement. Ben drags Charlie off to their hotel, and while Ben is trying to find the keyhole, Edna Purviance makes her first historic appearance in a Chaplin film. Wife of the head waiter, she has a hotel room opposite the two tipplers.

Chaplin's interest in her charm fades when her obtuse husband appears. After a dispute with Ben, he seeks new lodgings. But the married couple, too, have been dissatisfied with the restaurant service and take a room in the same hotel as Charlie. Preparing to turn in, he does everything wrong, tries to pour water out of the telephone and 'hangs out' his trousers from the open window.

Charlie is busy in the bathroom when the young wife's dog, pursued by the fair one herself in pyjamas, wanders into his bedroom with his mistress's slipper. Charlie comes in, and she has to hide under the bed. Charlie discovers her and pilots her back to her own room. At that moment her husband returns from a short promenade, Charlie tries to hide in their bed but is discovered and, threatened by a revolver, has to take an acrobatic leap through the open window. He returns to his own room where his friend Ben has now turned up; has a tussle with him, and finally ends up in the bathwater.

Originally Chaplin shot a brief introduction, which he entitled 'The Grand Final of the Broken Head Band Concert'. In it he conducts a brass band and is driven from the podium by a shower of rotten eggs, etc. But when *A Night Out* had its première this fragment was omitted. Nevertheless it is a very funny piece of pantomime. Together with *The Cure,* this film can be called Chaplin's least 'teetotaletarian' opus. Its virtues lie in its acrobatics and in a drastically comic situation. Ben Turpin's contribution is important; his only other major role in a Chaplin film was in *Carmen.*

38 The Champion (2 reel)

FIRST NIGHT 11 Mar 1915
ALTERNATIVE TITLES Champion Charlie, Battling Charlie
MAIN FRENCH TITLE Charlot Boxeur
DIRECTOR AND SCRIPTWRITER Charlie Chaplin
ACTORS Chaplin (challenger), Bud Jamison (world champion),
Lloyd Bacon (trainer), Edna Purviance (his daughter),
Leo White (dishonest better), 'Broncho' Billy Anderson
(enthusiastic fan at the ringside), Carl Stockdale.
Billy Armstrong, Paddy McGuire (sparring partners),
Ben Turpin (salesman in the beret)

Charlie and his faithful chum, a bulldog, chance to pass by a training camp where a boxing partner is required 'who can take a beating'. Just as he is thinking of applying for the job, he finds a horseshoe: a good omen. He picks it up. Sitting on the sparring partners' bench he sees one sparring partner after another knocked out by the local champion, and before undergoing his own baptism of fire stuffs the horseshoe into his glove. It works miracles. The champion is knocked out and driven out of the camp, and his trainer, beaming with pride and joy, accepts Charlie instead. He begins to prepare him for the big fight—against the world champion.

During his training a shady character puts in an appearance and tries to bribe Charlie to lie down in the World Championship match, but Charlie makes him regret his bid. While training, Charlie has also met and fallen in love with the trainer's daughter, who returns his feelings.

It is the day of the big fight. In his dressing room Charlie takes a fond farewell of his dog and goes out to meet his fate. The fight turns into a hilarious ballet—a technique already used in some of the training scenes—and it is perhaps the most exquisite parody of a boxing match ever seen on film. The boxers alternately chase each other round the ring, fall into each other's arms, and collapse on the floor.

The Champion, 1915.

Just as things are looking most critical for Charlie his faithful bulldog intervenes, plunges his teeth into the seat of the champion's pants and exposes him helpless to Charlie's last effort. Both boxers go out for the count, but Charlie is first to stagger to his feet and is declared the new champion. And of course gets the girl. *The Champion* is without question one of the gems in his collection.

39 In the Park (2 reel)

FIRST NIGHT 18 Mar 1915
ALTERNATIVE TITLES Charlie on the Spree,
Charlie in the Park
MAIN FRENCH TITLE Charlot dans le Park
DIRECTOR AND SCRIPTWRITER Charlie Chaplin
ACTORS Chaplin (stroller in the park), Edna Purviance
(nanny), Leo White (amorous gentleman), Margie Reiger

(the object of his tender passion), Bud Jamison (Edna's admirer), Billy Armstrong (thieving hobo), Lloyd Bacon (hot dog man), Ernest van Pelt (policeman)

Charlie, strolling in the park, comes across a pair of lovers on a bench and intervenes in their flirtations—a copy of his scene in *Twenty Minutes of Love*. But he soon withdraws. A tramp steals the girl's handbag, but when he tries to pick Charlie's pocket is himself robbed of his cigarettes and matches. Edna is being courted by her chubby swain, but while he is away buying her a hot dog Charlie appears. Edna is cool; her partner reappears, and once again Charlie has to withdraw. He rescues the hot dog man from a thug and manages to snatch a number of sausages with the aid of his walking stick. Again he meets the tramp, but when the latter tries to take his sausages Charlie filches the stolen handbag out of his pocket.

The handbag passes from hand to hand, it is sold by Charlie to Edna's boyfriend, stolen by the thief, taken charge of by the policeman, and then recovered surreptitiously by Charlie, who thereupon hands it over to the delighted Edna. But the rightful owner is displeased with her boyfriend who has not been able to protect her against theft, and the latter, in a fit of despair, goes off to drown himself in the lake. When he hesitates, Charlie, at his request, helps him, and on the arrival of the rest of the company sees to it that both the policeman and Edna's friend go the same way.

The Jitney Elopement, 1915, with Edna Purviance. In center is Lloyd Bacon.

Exit Charlie with Edna. A brick-throwing battle forms part of the action, and the whole style of this one-reeler is a temporary reversion to the Keystone epoch.

40   The Jitney Elopement (2 reel)

FIRST NIGHT 1 April 1915
ALTERNATIVE TITLES Married in Haste, Charlie's Elopement
MAIN FRENCH TITLE Charlot Veut se Marier
DIRECTOR AND SCRIPTWRITER Charlie Chaplin
ACTORS Chaplin (vagabond in love), Edna Purviance (girl),
Fred Goodwins (her father), Leo White (her millionaire
suitor Count de He-Ha), Paddy McGuire (head waiter),
Lloyd Bacon (footman), Carl Stockdale, Ernest van Pelt
and Bud Jamison (policemen)

Edna's father wants her to marry a wealthy count who has asked for her hand, but she is secretly in love with Charlie, who is standing outside her window. She writes him a note, asking him to help her. Charlie dresses up as the count, who is not personally known to her father, pays a visit and is received with open arms. After dinner the real suitor turns up, Charlie is unmasked and shown the door.

The father, the count and Edna take a trip in a car to cool off, and the couple are left alone in the park to 'make up their minds'. But here too Charlie turns up, drives his rival away with blows and sitting on the branch of a tree declares his love to Edna. Father and suitor return to the attack, but are driven off; then three policemen put in an appearance and Edna and Charlie flee to the suitor's parked car, an old taxi which runs on a slot meter.

The others pursue them in a police car, they drive through a police road block and after a wild chase Charlie crashes the car, causing their pursuers to drive over the edge of a pier into the canal. After which the two lovers go to the nearest clergyman.

41   The Tramp (2 reel)

FIRST NIGHT 11 Mar 1915
ALTERNATIVE TITLE Charlie the Hobo
MAIN FRENCH TITLE Charlot Vagabond
DIRECTOR AND SCRIPTWRITER Charlie Chaplin

ACTORS Chaplin (tramp), Fred Goodwins (farmer),
Edna Purviance (his daughter), Paddy McGuire (farmhand),
Lloyd Bacon (Edna's fiancé), Leo White, Bud Jamison
and Ernest van Pelt (sinister hobos)

Charlie is on the road. When he settles down to eat his lunch
another tramp appears from behind a tree and manages to swap
the sandwiches in his bundle for a brick, leaving Charlie to eat
grass. A farmer's daughter, who is busy counting her money, is
attacked by the same tramp; but Charlie comes to her aid and with
the brick in his bundle sorts the situation out. The tramp receives
assistance from two of his mates, but once again Charlie is master
of the situation and drives all three of them into a nearby lake.

The girl, grateful, invites Charlie to her father's farm where he
is given food and offered work to pay for it. As a farmhand he is a
failure. He sticks the pitchfork into another labourer, causes a
sack of flour to drop onto the farmer and tries to milk a cow by
pulling her tail.

Meanwhile the villains are preparing to break into the house.
Climbing a ladder up to the bedroom they are met by Charlie,
armed with a heavy club, and by the farmer equipped with a shotgun. They flee, pursued by Charlie, who receives a shot in the leg.
Charlie is declared a hero. Nursed by the family, he gets into the
daughter's good graces. But when her fiancé appears, Charlie
understands that he is superfluous. He writes her a pathetic farewell letter and then, lonely but optimistic, sets off for new adventures—the first of the tramp's famous exits in this style.

The Tramp constitutes one of the milestones in Chaplin's
development. Here, for the first time, his vagabond appears clearly
delineated, a figure in whom aggressiveness blends with pathos; a
little fellow who appeals to the viewer's pity and sympathy and
who under his rags conceals the gentleman and citizen of the
world. It is a film which still preserves all its freshness today.

42 By the Sea (1 reel)

FIRST NIGHT 29 Apl 1915
ALTERNATIVE TITLE Charlie's Day Out
MAIN FRENCH TITLE Charlot à la Plage
DIRECTOR AND SCRIPTWRITER Charlie Chaplin
ACTORS Chaplin (lovesick idler), Billy Armstrong (gentle-
man on holiday), Margie Reiger (his lady love),

Edna Purviance (the young wife), Bud Jamison (her husband), Carl Stockdale (policeman). The statement that Ben Turpin plays a part in this film appears to be incorrect.

This is Chaplin's last one-reeler, apart from his 1918 film *The Bond*, made for the Liberty Loan Committee. It was also the first film for Essanay made in Majestic Studio at Los Angeles. Really this is no more than a sketch; yet a remarkable one, inasmuch as Chaplin returns to his earlier tough Keystone comedy style.

The scene is a bathing resort on a windy day. Billy says farewell to his lady friend and wanders down to the beach, where Charlie also arrives after a spectacular slip up on a banana skin, by way of introduction. Both have fixed their hats on with rubber bands and in the gale Charlie and Billy, after various 'hat tricks', manage to get entangled, become furious with each other and tangle at close quarters.

Edna, whose husband (Bud) is faithfully waiting for her on a bench in the park, witnesses a comic dance, using a life-buoy. Charlie then flirts with Edna, is reconciled with Billy and there is a superb scene beside an ice cream stall, where Bud, who is also hankering after an ice, comes to grief and a general fight breaks out. Charlie approaches Edna, is driven away by the jealous Bud, and then tries to flirt with Billy's girl on a bench down by the beach, where they all end up, and where Bud and Billy try to settle matters with Charlie. He escapes by upsetting the bench. The film's good qualities lie in its swift tempo and acrobatics.

43 Work (2 reel)

FIRST NIGHT 21 June 1915
ALTERNATIVE TITLES The Paperhanger, Charlie at Work, Only a Working Man, The Plumber
MAIN FRENCH TITLE Charlot Apprenti
DIRECTOR AND SCRIPTWRITER Charlie Chaplin
ACTORS Chaplin (decorator's apprentice), Charles Insley (his boss), Edna Purviance (housemaid), Billy Armstrong (householder), Marta Golden (his wife), Leo White (suitor to the daughter of the house), Paddy McGuire (a craftsman)

Work is one of the films which have been played about with, and whose original material has been used in a later film *Triple Trouble* (see chapter on spurious 'Chaplin' films).

Charlie and his boss, the house painter and wallpaper hanger, are on their way to a job, and it is Charlie who has to be the cart-horse. The action begins with a very funny scene where the two men have to mount a slope and Charlie is left hanging in the air on the shafts. Hurtling down the slope the cart and its crew just miss being crushed by a streetcar. Meanwhile the house where the wallpaper is to be hung is in an uproar. The paterfamilias is complaining because he cannot get his breakfast; his wife is bawl-ing at the maid. Finally Charlie arrives exhausted, having acquired an extra passenger on the cart. Work can now begin. Not however without complications. When the gas stove in the kitchen explodes Charlie offers his services to repair it, leaving his boss up to his ears in glue. The whole dining room becomes one big slippery battlefield and Charlie withdraws to wallpaper the maid's bed-room. The results are not brilliant. Charlie prefers to air his sor-rows to Edna on the edge of the bed and to dream of the future.

The wife has a clandestine lover. In the middle of it all he pays her a visit, bringing her some flowers. She introduces him as the workmen's boss. Pretending to intervene in their work, he is beaten up by Charlie. The husband realises he is an imposter. General hullaballoo follows, with shots being fired by the husband.

Just as Charlie is fleeing, the gas stove explodes so violently that the whole house is blown sky high, his boss ends up in the bath-water and all the others among the ruins. Charlie's face appears out of the oven, only to beat a hasty retreat behind its door. Exactly the same scene forms the finale of *Triple Trouble*, released three years later.

Work is dominated by effective slapstick and a couple of details of genuinely Chaplinesque pantomime. The wallpaper-hanging scene was copied by him long afterwards and developed into a sketch in *A King in New York* (1957).

44   A Woman (2 reel)

FIRST NIGHT 12 July 1915
ALTERNATIVE TITLES The Perfect Lady,
Charlie the Perfect Lady
MAIN FRENCH TITLE Mam'zelle Charlot
DIRECTOR AND SCRIPTWRITER Charlie Chaplin
ACTORS Chaplin (a gallant gentleman, who is obliged to
dress up as a woman), Edna Purviance (daughter of the
house), Charles Insley (her father), Marta Golden

(her mother), Margie Reiger (her father's lady friend),
Billy Armstrong (the new friend in the house), Leo White
(idler in the park)

The family—father, mother and daughter—are taking a Sunday
walk in the park. They sit down on a bench, where the ladies drop
off to sleep. Meanwhile the father spots a flirtatious girl on another
bench and makes advances. While he is fetching her some lemon-
ade, Charlie, idling in the park, has found the same target for his
feelings and makes crude approaches. He is driven off by the paterfamilias, who walks off with the girl. She entices him into a game
of blind man's buff, promising a kiss if he can catch her. Meanwhile Charlie has found company on the bench, in the form of
two other gentlemen both in their Sunday best. Naturally a quarrel starts. Again he meets up with the father, who is now wandering
about with a bandage over his eyes, searching for the girl. Charlie
leads him to the brink of the pond, pushes him in with his walking stick, as he does one of his acquaintances from the other bench
who happens by. The two gentlemen struggle ashore, become
friends over a glass of beer, whereupon the father invites his new-
found friend to come to his house. But before that can happen
Charlie has already inveigled himself into the good graces of the
two tired ladies. Mother and daughter both fall for him, and Charlie is invited home to dinner.

Dinner is interrupted by the arrival of the two gentlemen.
Attacked by both of them, Charlie is in a bad way, loses his trousers and, unable to get out of the house, flees up to Edna's room.
In her cupboard he finds clothes and furs, and dresses up as an
attractive woman. On Edna's advice he even shaves off his moustache. Lady Charlie presents herself as a college friend of the
daughter of the house. Immediately she charms both the gentlemen, who make approaches but are roughly rejected. The friend,
now his rival, is shown the door by the father of the family, who
falls on his knees before the beauty, only to discover that the lady
is none other than the detestable Charlie. Edna's prayers avail
nothing. The father, at first seemingly inclined to yield to Charlie's
threats to tell his wife about the whole escapade, flies into a rage
and Charlie is thrown out.

In 1915, *A Woman* was a controversial film. Its transvestite
theme, in which a man dressed as a woman is made love to—
admittedly in an innocent manner—was a delicate one. At all
events the Swedish censors knew their own mind. When the film
came up before them in 1917, they banned it completely. Three

years later another distributor tried to release a much shortened version. But the censor banned that too. Not until 1931 did the censor pass it.

45 The Bank (2 reel)

FIRST NIGHT 9 Aug 1915
ALTERNATIVE TITLES Charlie at the Bank, Charlie Detective
MAIN FRENCH TITLE Charlot à la Banque
DIRECTOR AND SCRIPTWRITER Charlie Chaplin
ACTORS Chaplin (janitor in a bank), Edna Purviance
(typist—his heart-throb), Carl Stockdale (cashier),
Charles Insley (bank manager), Leo White (client),
Billy Armstrong (Charlie's workmate), Fred Goodwins
(doorkeeper), Bud Jamison (client of the bank and leader of
a gang of crooks), John Rand, Lloyd Bacon, Frank J. Coleman
and Paddy McGuire (crooks), Wesley Ruggles,
Carrie Clark Ward

Charlie, janitor at the bank, makes an impressive entry, goes down into the vaults, opens the safe and hangs up his outdoor clothes inside it. All is ready for him to do his day's cleaning. After doing one room he sweeps all the rubbish into the next, leaving his mate to do two men's work. (An episode repeated in a new version in *The Gold Rush*, when Charlie sweeps up snow from cottage door to cottage door.) He handles his mop skilfully so as to collide with everyone.

The cashier Charles, fiancé of the typist Edna, is to celebrate his birthday. She has bought him a present. But when Charlie catches sight of the packet with 'To Charles with Love' written on it, he imagines the present is for himself. Radiant with happiness he gets her a flower with a card attached: 'To Edna with love—Charlie', and leaves it on her table. But soon his error becomes painfully obvious. Charlie sees Edna throw his flower into the wastepaper basket.

Depressed, he sits down in a corner and drops off to sleep. He dreams that a gang of burglars have broken into the bank. They overwhelm the manager and go down into the vaults where they overcome Edna and the cashier. But Charlie rushes to their assistance, defeats the burglars, shuts them up in the vault and carries off Edna, who has fainted, to the manager's office—where the cowardly cashier has hidden himself. The last of the burglars is dealt with, the manager kicks out the useless cashier, and Charlie, hero of the occasion, takes Edna into his arms. But then he wakes up to find he is sitting caressing his floor mop. Once again, the dreary reality of everyday life...

The Bank is one of Chaplin's most popular films from 1915, offering as it does a well-composed story with room both for ingenious comic situations and sentimental elements. It shows Chaplin at the height of his form.

46 Shanghaied (2 reel)

FIRST NIGHT 4 Oct 1915
ALTERNATIVE TITLES Charlie the Sailor,
Charlie on the Ocean
MAIN FRENCH TITLE Charlot Marine
DIRECTOR AND SCRIPTWRITER Charlie Chaplin
ACTORS Chaplin (tramp), Edna Purviance (daughter of the shipowner), Wesley Ruggles (shipowner), John Rand (captain), Bud Jamison ('the other man'), Leo White, Paddy McGuire and Fred Goodwins (shanghaied seamen), Billy Armstrong (ship's cook), Lawrence A. Bowes (member of the crew)

A cargo ship is to set out on her last voyage. The shipowner wants the insurance money and has agreed with the captain to scuttle her at sea. All they need is a crew. Charlie, a tramp who has fallen in love with the shipowner's young daughter Edna, comes down to the harbour. There he is grabbed by the skipper and promises to help him shanghai some seamen. He hides in a barrel while the captain fetches one seaman after another, enticing them on board by the prospect of a drink. Charlie hits them on the head with a club, whereupon they 'sign on'. In the end he is given the treatment himself and is carried down into the hold. The newcomers are brutally put to work, but sacks are loaded under Charlie's direction in such a fashion that both the captain and 'the mate' are caught on the hook and, with several of the seamen, are repeatedly dipped in the sea.

After the ship has put to sea it turns out there is a stowaway on board; namely, the shipowner's daughter. Secretly she has followed 'her' Charlie, leaving behind a letter to her father. Panic-stricken at the thought of the dynamite on board, he chases after the ship in a motorboat.

Shaghaied, 1915. The forceful recruiters are Bud Jamison and John Rand.

Meanwhile Charlie has been given the task of assisting in the galley, where he causes confusion, washing plates in the soup, etcetera. There is a notable piece of highly gracious pantomime (corresponding to the one in the bathing hut in *The Cure*) and later a balancing act when Charlie is serving dinner in the saloon and a full gale suddenly blows up. Certain scenes may be regarded as preliminary studies for *The Immigrant*—both the milieu and the pattern of the action are extremely similar, eg, the sliding of the plates to and fro on the dining table.

Finally Charlie falls victim to seasickness. Finding his way down into the hold he comes across Edna, who has hidden in a sack. The skipper and the mate come down. From their hiding place Charlie and Edna see them light the fuses to the dynamite. After which the captain and his mate get into a lifeboat. But Charlie, the lethal charge in his hands, comes up on deck and flings it into the lifeboat, which blows up. At that moment the shipowner's motorboat arrives. Charlie and Edna go on board. Charlie is rejected as a son-in-law, and pretends to commit suicide. He jumps overboard, but surfaces again on the other side of the boat, climbs aboard, and with a well-directed kick sends his father-in-law flying.

47 A Night in the Show (2 reel)

FIRST NIGHT 20 Nov 1915
ALTERNATIVE TITLE Charlie at the Show
MAIN FRENCH TITLE Charlot au Music-Hall
DIRECTOR AND SCRIPTWRITER Charlie Chaplin
ACTORS Chaplin (double role as Mr Pest a tipsy gentleman
in the stalls, and as the even drunker tramp Mr Rowdy,
in the gallery), Charlotte Mineau (Edna's neighbour in the
stalls), Dee Lampton (the fat young man in the box),
Leo White (conjuror and member of the audience in the stalls
and in the box), Wesley Ruggles (member of the audience
in the gallery), John Rand (the conductor), James T. Kelly
and Paddy McGuire (members of the orchestra), May White
(the snake-charmer, also the fat lady who falls into the
fountain), Bud Jamison (the big singer, also Edna's husband
in the stalls), Phyllis Allen, Fred Goodwins and Charles
Insley (members of the audience)

Mr Pest, a gentleman who has had one over the eight, makes his entry into a music hall of the traditional English type. He has some difficulty in finding his right seat in the stalls and several times has to change it. Finally he ends up in the front row where he tangles with the short-sighted conductor, whom he pushes into the orchestra pit. Charlie is chucked out, taking with him some of the wind instruments as he goes. In the foyer he pushes a fat lady into the fountain; then returns and finds a seat next to Edna.

Meanwhile, up in the gallery, Mr Rowdy (Chaplin's other part) is beginning to become troublesome. He pours the contents of a bottle of beer down over the heads of Mr Pest and Edna. Edna's husband comes in and Charlie has to change seats—with fatal results. Charlie and the husband find they are holding each other's hands. He enters a box, where he sits down on Leo White's hat.

Charlie is becoming steadily more and more aggressive. He plucks the feathers out of the hat of a woman next to him, makes his way on to the stage where he engages in a wrestling match with a fat harem dancer; and when two singers, Dot & Dash, appear, he goes into double action. As Mr Rowdy he flings eggs and tomatoes at them from the gallery, and as Mr Pest he closes Mr Dash's mouth with a pie.

A snake-charmer appears. One of her snakes approaches the somnolent Mr Pest while other snakes wriggle down into the orchestra pit, causing panic. Later during a fire-eating act, Mr Rowdy, seized with a desire to put out the fire, fetches the firehose and aims it at stage and stalls. Charlie, finding himself the target, decides to beat a retreat under the protection of his umbrella. Finally he leaves the music hall, now in a state of utter chaos.

The action of this film was based on the music hall act he had played in when he was with Fred Karno, an act known in England under the name of *Mumming Birds*, and later in America in 1913, under the title *A Night in an English Music Hall*. It was while taking part in it that he had been noticed by Mack Sennett's spotter. Indirectly it had been his ticket of entry to Hollywood. It is one of Chaplin's most eventful two-reelers, with pantomime episodes following close upon one another.

48   Carmen (4 reel)

FIRST NIGHT 22 Apl 1916
ALTERNATIVE TITLE Charlie Chaplin's Burlesque on Carmen
MAIN FRENCH TITLE Charlot Joue Carmen
DIRECTOR AND SCRIPTWRITER Charlie Chaplin
ACTORS Chaplin (Don José, the lieutenant of the guard),
Edna Purviance (Carmen), Ben Turpin (Renandados, a
smuggler), Jack Henderson (Lilas Pastia, the leader of the
smugglers), Leo White (an officer of the guard), John Rand
(Escamillo, the toreador), May White (Frasquita),
Bud Jamison (a soldier of the guard), Wesley Ruggles
(a vagabond), Lawrence A. Bowes, Frank J. Coleman

The film begins with the leader of the smugglers, Lilas Pastia, landing his men on a rocky coast with their contraband. They go up to a camp in the mountains, where the smuggler Ben Turpin has an amorous intermezzo with the plump gypsy girl Frasquita.

The cocky guards lieutenant Don José—called Darn Hosiery in the film—is introduced. Pastia tries to bribe him. He refuses, so Pastia sends the pretty gypsy girl Carmen to see what she can do. Another officer, Escamillo, is in love with her. Carmen charms Don José, entices him away from the coastguard station, so that the contraband can secretly be smuggled into the town.

At a feast in a tavern the triangular plot thickens. Carmen makes fun of Don José. Unresigned to losing her, he fights a comic duel with the commander of the guard, another of Carmen's admirers. This duel is one of Chaplin's very finest scenes, a phenomenal ballet suite of many phases. Don José kills the officer and in despair turns to Carmen, who has now dropped him in favour of the heroic bullfighter Escamillo. Meantime Ben Turpin has been enjoying an amour with Frasquita, and in the sub-plot, where he plays the central role, there is a wild fight between Frasquita and Carmen.

Don José, who has killed himself, comes back to life. It was only arena, where she is waiting outside the wall for Escamillo to come out after his bullfight and he takes her by surprise. When she again rejects him, Don José, seized with fury, draws his dagger and stabs her in the breast. Escamillo, horrified, finds them both lying on the ground—but then, suddenly, the tragedy is interrupted. Don José, who has killed himself, comes back to life. It was only a stage-dagger. He kicks Escamillo back into the arena, and, as far as we can judge, gets his beloved Carmen, who has also happily come back to life.

In one scene, the one where he watches Escamillo riding off to the arena, Chaplin oddly enough is wearing his classic bowler. Otherwise the costumes are 'authentically Spanish'.

Chaplin based this film partly on the traditional action of Bizet's opera, and partly on the film of *Carmen* which had come out that same year (1915), starring the singer Geraldine Farrar, and of which it is a parody. Unfortunately, the film hardly came up to Chaplin's expectations. There are too many irrelevant scenes; the tempo is uneven; and the whole film hangs together very poorly. This was not Chaplin's fault. Originally he had planned *Carmen* as a two-reeler. It was the Essanay company which made a mess of it—as it also did with *Triple Trouble* (see 'Spurious' Chaplin Films).

At the beginning of 1915 Chaplin had not been allowed to complete his planned feature film *Life*. The company had been afraid of its length. But now Essanay had changed its mind, and wanted to extend *Carmen*, which was in the middle of shooting, into a four-reeler; something which could not be done until after the New Year 1916, when Chaplin had left Essanay and gone over to Mutual. Essanay immediately got busy piecing together its four-reeler. This it did partly with the aid of reserve footage already shot, and partly by introducing new sequences. One of the most faithful of Chaplin's ex-colleagues, Leo White, also had a talent for directing and was given the task of extending the story. Ben Turpin had to become a second star in the action. As for the audiences, they were only too happy to be conned.

Anyone who sees this film today will hardly guess that the smuggler Turpin and his escapades have been stuck on afterwards. What he may notice, however, is that Chaplin and Turpin *never actually meet* in any of the scenes. Chaplin was furious at the vandalisation and sued his former company, without success. On 22 April 1916 the four-reeler *Carmen* had its premiére.

49 Police! (2 reel)

FIRST NIGHT 27 Mar 1916
ALTERNATIVE TITLES Charlie the Burglar, Housebreaker
MAIN FRENCH TITLE Charlot Cambrioleur
DIRECTOR AND SCRIPTWRITER Charlie Chaplin
ACTORS Chaplin (tramp), Edna Purviance (daughter of the house), Wesley Ruggles (gaolbird and thief), James T. Kelly (drunk who has had his pockets picked; also a vagabond), Leo White (a fruitseller; also a superintendent of a night shelter; and a policeman), John Rand (policeman), Fred Goodwins (bogus preacher), Billy Armstrong (shady character), Bud Jamison (another shady character), Frank J. Coleman

Charlie has come out of gaol and is returning to the 'cruel world outside'. Instantly he is accosted by a minister of religion, who exhorts him to stick to the straight and narrow. Falling in with a drunken gentleman, he resists the temptation to pinch his watch, only to be promptly 'cured' when—after a quarrel with a fruit-seller—he discovers that the 'pastor' has himself pocketed it. The next clergyman he meets gets a brusque reception. Unfortunately, when chasing him away, Charlie chances to knock over a police-man. And instantly the hue and cry is up. A thief, lurking in a doorway, rushes out and tries to go through Charlie's pockets—but instead it is Charlie who filches a coin from the thief's. Where-upon he recognises him as a former gaol-mate.

Originally this coin was to have gained Charlie entry to the night shelter, where he was to have been given a bed. But the long night shelter sequence which followed was never included in *Police!*—why? The whole sequence, including those parts of it which are used in *Police!*, originally belonged to *Life*, the long film which was to have been a serious study, seen from Chaplin's satiri-

81

cal angle, of the lives led by society's misfits. The footage was preserved and utilised by Chaplin in this section of *Police!*

But after Chaplin had completed the film—and under circumstances of some tension had left Essanay—the larger and more valuable part of the night shelter sequence was 'borrowed' for inclusion in the film *Triple Trouble*, which made its dubious appearance two years later

If this sequence could be edited back, *Police!* would be greatly improved. Some eight-millimeter enthusiasts must certainly have done just this, and I myself have felt tempted. But in the 'official' version of *Police!* the action goes on airily with the thief prevailing on Charlie to join in breaking and entering a house occupied by a girl and her sick mother. Charlie, equipped with a club, is sent ahead to smash a window. When a policeman appears he knocks him down, and the two thieves, realising that the door is open anyway, slip inside. There they find plenty of booty. But Charlie's clumsiness wakes the girl, who rings for the police. Charlie's aggressive companion wants to look for other valuables on the second floor; but Charlie's heart is softened by the girl's imploring appeals not to disturb her sick mother, and he successfully battles with his colleague.

The police turn up, the thief runs off, and the girl saves Charlie by claiming he is her husband. Before leaving he is given a tip; but outside waits another policeman who has a bone to pick with him. Once more the hunt is on.

Even in its final abbreviated form *Police!* became one of Chaplin's most popular Essanay films, and it has often been included in Chaplin seasons. In satirical guise its crude depiction of a certain social milieu has captured something of the realities of Chaplin's own slum world in those days. The interior of the night shelter can be seen as an elaborate forerunner of *The Kid*, shot six years later. Amid all the farce the streak of pathos, lost sight of since *The Tramp*, reappears. All lists give *Police!* a later date than *Carmen*, as it was completed after that film. But the manipulations with *Carmen* delayed its release, and *Police!* had already had its first night a month earlier.

50 Triple Trouble (2 reel)

FIRST NIGHT 11 Aug 1918
MAIN FRENCH TITLE Les Avatars de Charlot
DIRECTOR AND SCRIPTWRITER Chaplin in 1915, albeit for

Chaplin as Don Jose in *Carmen*, 1916,
with Edna Purviance in the title role.

other films. New complementary footage shot by
Essanay in 1918, edited by Leo White
ACTORS Chaplin (the kitchen boy), Edna Purviance
(housemaid), Billy Armstrong (cook, also the ragged thief),
Leo White (German master spy), James T. Kelly,
Bud Jamison, Wesley Ruggles, Albert Austin

The action is supposed to occur during World War I. Charlie takes
a job as a kitchen boy in a house owned by an inventor, Colonel
Nutt (in some copies called Professor Potash). This character has
made an invention of military importance, an explosive device
which is attracting the attention of German spies. But when the
head of the German espionage pays the inventor a visit, he will not
sell and the German is shown the door. By this time Charlie, too,
has managed to get the sack after causing the usual chaos and confusion in the kitchens.

He goes to the night shelter (taken from *Life* and the original
version of *Police!*) and there finds himself among a gang of sinister
ne'erdowells, who make it utterly impossible for him to sleep. The
funniest scene in the film is where Charlie lies feet-about under
his blanket in order to keep an eye on a light-fingered ragamuffin,
whose greed brings its own reward. The same scene in a new version was used in *The Gold Rush* (in the hut) and it is also possible to trace the tree scene in *Shoulder Arms* back to it.

The master spy hires a low character—identical with the one
in *Police!*—to steal the professor's invention; and this fellow in
his turn links up with Charlie. Here the scenes from *Police!* are
doubled. In that film the couple break into the house where the
girl is living with her sick mother. In *Triple Trouble* the house,
though this time it belongs to the professor, is identical both outside and inside. But there are some newly shot scenes of the police,
summoned by the professor, swarming about.

Charlie has very little to do with the finale—for obvious reasons,
he was not available for the shootings. But a couple of shots showing him taking to his heels (drawn from *Police!*) have been slipped
in before the big bang, when the invention explodes and the entire
house is blown sky-high.

In the final scene Charlie's head appears in the oven (from
Work) contemplating the scene of destruction all about him. Even
worse havoc was caused by the falsification, no matter how clever,
of a Chaplin film.

The Mutual Period

If Chaplin's time with Essanay is regarded as a time of transition during which he was given greater freedom than he had enjoyed with Keystone to find his own way forward, the years 1916–17 with Mutual were the period of Chaplin's great success on a broad front, not merely in one or another individual film. Once again, his salary was multiplied several times over. Now he had unlimited resources to work with. He took with him to Mutual the élite of the Essanay group (among them Edna Purviance, Leo White and Lloyd Bacon) and now added to his private 'stable' such future mainstays as that immense villain Eric Campbell, the versatile Henry Bergman, and Albert Austin the butler.

More time was now devoted to each film. Greater attention was paid to sets. The gags were introduced more subtly into the action. Above all, Chaplin was now in a position to introduce satire and leave room for the pathetic streak. The tramp figure was to be introduced into a social context. The foundations were now laid for the philosophy of life which permeates Chaplin's later full-length feature films.

Twelve two-reelers were shot, eight of them during 1916 and only four in 1917. All are gems of the art of farce. The films were shot in a newly built studio, The Lone Star, at 1025 Lillian Way in Hollywood. Here, at the end of March 1916, Chaplin got busy. The results were to delight a whole world of movie-goers and even half a century later they make good viewing. With his Mutual films Chaplin conquered a world-wide public.

51   The Floorwalker (8 reel)

FIRST NIGHT 15 May 1916
ALTERNATIVE TITLE The Store
MAIN FRENCH TITLE Charlot Chef de Rayon
DIRECTOR AND SCRIPTWRITER Charlie Chaplin
ACTORS Chaplin (tramp), Eric Campbell (store manager),

Edna Purviance (his secretary), Lloyd Bacon (shop inspector), Albert Austin (shop assistant), Leo White (elegant French-style customer), Charlotte Mineau (the beautiful tall house-detective), James T. Kelly (liftboy)

The manager of a small store receives some very bad financial news in a letter, and summons his shop inspector. Meanwhile, downstairs in the store itself, quite a few things are going on. Charlie has come in and is on the loose among goods and assistants. Fleeing from the store detective, he happens to appear on the office floor where, together with the manager, the inspector—Charlie's spit image—has just plundered the safe and then knocked out his colleague.

The confrontation between them is a scene of magnificent humour. At first Charlie imagines he is standing in front of a mirror; then he notices that his reflection is holding a bag (containing the money), while he himself is carrying a walking stick. (Seventeen years later the Marx Brothers copied this mirror sketch in *Duck Soup*.) The criminal store inspector proposes to Charlie that they swap clothes and identities. A banknote helps to convince him.

The store detective tracks him down; but then the false Charlie with the bag appears, he grabs him instead, and an unsuspecting assistant hands over the ownerless bag to Charlie, who suddenly finds himself wealthy.

By now the boss has come to his senses. Rushing down he attacks Charlie, who just has time to fling the bag up the moving staircase. Here it is found by the boss's secretary and afterwards taken back by the boss, who slips down with his booty. But there are many claimants to the bag. One of them is a client. With the detective's eye upon him—a female detective is also involved—it is more than the boss dares do to hinder Charlie's retreat up to the office. Here the boss and Charlie again settle matters between them in a struggle in which the entire personnel as well as the police gradually become involved. The film ends with the manager being arrested as he is trying to make good his escape via the lift.

The Floorwalker contains some original Chaplinesque gags in its store scenes. His use of the moving staircase for farcical purposes is positively virtuosic. 'Why didn't *I* ever think of that' Mack Sennett is said to have exclaimed angrily when he saw the film. Another notable scene is the one in which Charlie, in the midst of his struggle with the store manager, dances a ballet in honour of the dollar.

52   The Fireman (2 reel)

FIRST NIGHT 12 June 1916
MAIN FRENCH TITLE Charlot Pompier
DIRECTOR AND SCRIPTWRITER Charlie Chaplin
ACTORS Chaplin (fireman), Edna Purviance (the girl),
Lloyd Bacon (her father), Eric Campbell (foreman of the
fire brigade), Leo White (owner of a house which burns
down), Albert Austin, John Rand, James T. Kelly
and Frank J. Coleman (firemen)

Charlie, a fireman, is the scapegoat of the fire station. When the
alarm sounds he is always last to turn out. Then, while waiting on
his fellow-firemen at dinner, he reacts to it so promptly that he
spills soup all over the fire captain. But it was only a street fish-
monger ringing his bell.

The fire captain is visited by a houseowner whose pretty young
daughter he is in love with. The father is planning to set fire to his
own house in order to get the insurance money and talks his pros-
pective son-in-law into not intervening. The latter promises not to
do so, and the father goes off home to put fire to the house. But his
daughter, knowing nothing of her father's plan, has been left
upstairs on the first storey.

Meanwhile another house happens to catch fire, and when no
one answers the phone its despairing owner rushes to the fire
station. Charlie, who is on duty, has been busy playing cards with
a colleague. In the end, however, he rouses the entire fire brigade
and drives off to the scene of the fire.

There he is met by the father who confesses in despair that he
has set fire to his own house, but that his daughter is in mortal
danger upstairs. Charlie has managed to lose the hose in the course
of his furious drive but flies to her rescue, climbs boldly up to her
window, saves her, and, apparently overcome by smoke, collapses.
He soon comes to, however, and the film ends with a tender scene
between the hero and the girl, who breaks off her engagement to
the captain of the fire brigade.

Characteristic of *The Fire* is its swift tempo and a whole series of
brilliant equilibristic feats. The fireman's ballet is one of the high-
lights. Likewise the rapid movements of the firemen up and down
the fire pole. On the other hand the film does not represent any
advance in Chaplin's development. Rather it is a regression to a
highly polished Keystone style.

Eric Campbell played one of his many
villain roles in *The Vagabond*, 1916.

53   The Vagabond (2 reel)

FIRST NIGHT 10 July 1916
MAIN FRENCH TITLE Charlot Musicien
DIRECTOR AND SCRIPTWRITER Charlie Chaplin
ACTORS Chaplin (street musician), Edna Purviance (waif
who has been picked up by a gypsy family), Eric Campbell
(gypsy chieftain), Leo White (old Jew; and also an old
gypsy woman), Lloyd Bacon (young artist), Charlotte Mineau
(Edna's mother), Albert Austin (trombonist), John Rand
(trumpeter and leader of a band), James T. Kelly and
Frank J. Coleman (musicians and gypsies)

We start with Chaplin's big shoes appearing in the lower swing
doorway of a bar. Coming into the bar the vagabond violinist tries
to compete with a group of German street musicians. He goes round
with his hat and reaps the harvest of their efforts—until they see

what is going on and Charlie, after a successful tussle, has to beat a hasty retreat.

Now he is on his way out to the peace and quiet of the countryside, where he meets the girl. Edna is standing washing her clothes outside a gypsy caravan. It transpires that as a child she was kidnapped by the gypsies, and that her mother, a society woman, has never ceased to grieve for her. She is being maltreated by the leader of the gypsies.

Charlie plays his violin to the girl, who becomes so excited by his ever faster rhythm that in the end she upsets the washtub. Interrupting their idyll, the gypsy chief gives the girl a whipping; but Charlie, indignant, seizes a club, climbs up into a tree, knocks

he Vagabond, 1916, Chaplin was a
: musician, and Edna Purviance
the waif he befriended.

out several of the gypsies and their chieftain, and flees with the girl in their caravan.

Now the couple have reached safety and are camping in idyllic surroundings. Charlie helps Edna with her toilette, which includes washing her face and delousing her, and then sends her off to fetch some more water. Near the spring a young artist has set up his easel. Much taken by the girl, he wants to paint her portrait. For Edna, too, its love at first sight. Poor Charlie realises he is unwanted. The romance he had envisaged has gone up in smoke.

Time passes. The artist's portrait of Edna is on display in an exhibition where it is discovered by some friends of Edna's family. Her mother is informed. Thanks to an unusual birthmark on her arm she recognises her long-lost daughter and tries to trace her.

Meanwhile Charlie has been trying in vain to recover lost ground—but no matter how great his artistic ambitions the competition is too strong. One day a chauffeur-driven car arrives on the scene. The mother and the artist have come to fetch the girl. It is an emotional moment. Charlie is offered money for what he has done, but scornfully rejects it. Sadly he watches the car drive off.

The Vagabond is unlike Chaplin's earlier films—except perhaps *The Tramp*—in being wholly dramatic in structure. There are few comic elements. Romance and pathos dominate, thus foreshadowing *The Kid* and *The Circus*, especially the latter with its emotional triangle. But *The Vagabond* is no more than a gifted preliminary study for the longer films of the twenties.

54   One AM (2 reel)

FIRST NIGHT 7 Aug 1916
MAIN FRENCH TITLE Charlot Rentre Tard
DIRECTOR AND SCRIPTWRITER Charlie Chaplin
ACTORS Chaplin (gentleman on a booze-up),
Albert Austin (taxi driver)

Another of Chaplin's 'odd' films, in which he appears for the first time in a one-man mime. Clad in evening dress and top hat he comes home late, decidedly the worse for drink. His passage from the sitting room up to his bedroom is a series of contretemps. When paying the taxi driver he has already run into trouble; unable to find the front door key he has had to climb in through the window, after which he has come out again with the key and entered through the door. After various equilibristic feats and a life-and-death struggle with a tigerskin mat, his cloak gets caught in a circular rotating table top, with the result that the brandy and soda siphon always remain tantalisingly out of reach. More acrobatics follow on the staircase, where he keeps slipping up in the most virtuosic manner and in the end is half knocked out by the pendulum of a clock. But the real crisis comes in the bedroom, where he is involved in a violent struggle with a collapsible wall-bed which behaves as if it were a living monster, perpetually frustrating his desire to turn in.

This long sequence is the film's highlight. Finally, Charlie resigns and takes refuge in the bath, an ending which has already suggested itself in an earlier film, *A Night Out*, and which was to recur in 1922 in *Pay Day*.

Charlie's struggles with a wall bed in *One A.M.*, 1916, represented his classic theme of man against machine.

55 The Count (2 reel)

FIRST NIGHT 4 Sept 1916
MAIN FRENCH TITLE Charlot et Le Comte
DIRECTOR AND SCRIPTWRITER Charlie Chaplin
ACTORS Chaplin (tailor's apprentice), Eric Campbell
(the master tailor), Edna Purviance (Miss Moneybags the
Heiress), Leo White (Count), May White (large fat lady),
Albert Austin (a guest), Charlotte Mineau (Edna's mummy),
James T. Kelly (footman), Leota Bryan (a young girl),
Loyal Underwood (a little old man of no stature),
Eva Thatcher (the cook), Frank J. Coleman (policeman and
guest in pierrot costume), Stanley Sanford, John Rand

Charlie the tailor's apprentice is measuring a young lady. Her measurements however prove problematic, as a tailor's dummy which happens to be standing behind her, also insists on being taken into account. The tailor comes in and sends Charlie away. He does some ironing, but unfortunately leaves the iron on the trousers of a count, which he ruins. Charlie gets the sack.

In the count's pockets the tailor finds a letter from Count Broko, in which he regrets he is unable to accept Miss Moneybags' invitation to a party. The tailor takes his chance and goes in his stead. What he does not know is that Charlie happens to have an acquaintance inside the house—namely the cook. So it happens that both visit the house at once. Charlie, of course, has to dine in the kitchen; but when the footman turns up (he too entertains tender feelings for the cook) Charlie takes refuge in a washing basket. A ring at the door, another of the cook's admirers, a police constable, enters and Charlie seeks a safer refuge in the lift which carries food up to the hall. Before long the policeman has to take Charlie's place in the washing basket.

The lift goes up to the hall. Charlie, peeping out through the curtain, is promptly discovered by the tailor, who thinks he is having hallucinations. But Charlie is real, and the tailor has to confess his secret. He begs Charlie to keep his mouth shut and to pretend to be the count's private secretary. Whereupon Charlie promptly presents himself as the count and the tailor as his secretary and becomes the heart and soul of the very mixed company.

At table he is seated beside the beautiful hostess, Edna, with the tailor on his other side. To Charlie the meal proves a source of infinite trouble. He struggles in vain with his spaghetti and takes so deep a bite into his water melon that it gets stuck in his ears.

Afterwards he is a great success on the dance floor, where he duels corybantically with the tailor and others.

Now the real count arrives on the scene, is told he has a double, and the party comes to an abrupt end. Charlie, who has been playfully ravaging the buffet with a game of golf, causes an uproar. Rushing away through the house he meets the count and only by the skin of his teeth does he escape the furious tailor who has somehow managed to get hold of a loaded pistol and is finally arrested by the policeman, while Charlie disappears out into the park. *The Count* is a two-reeler full of swift action. Charlie's demonstration dance is the highlight of its exquisitely accurate parody.

56   The Pawnshop (2 reel)

FIRST NIGHT 2 Oct 1916
MAIN FRENCH TITLE Charlot Chez l'Usurier
DIRECTOR AND SCRIPTWRITER Charlie Chaplin
ACTORS Chaplin (assistant in a pawnshop), Henry Bergman (the pawnbroker), Edna Purviance (his daughter), John Rand (other assistant in the shop), Albert Austin (the client, who wants to pawn his alarm clock), Wesley Ruggles (client who wants to pawn his ring), Eric Campbell (burglar), James T. Kelly (female client with the goldfish), Frank J. Coleman (policeman)

Charlie is an assistant in a pawnshop where he is competing with another assistant for the favours of the pawnbroker. Turning up late for work, Charlie begins frantically cleaning up. He tears his duster to shreds by getting it caught in an electric fan, and to his colleague's great annoyance first drops a ladder on his foot and then catches him in it and drags him backwards out of the shop. On the pavement Charlie demonstrates in the most magnificent manner how to use a ladder as a battering ram (reminiscent of his juggling with the punchballs during the training scenes in *The Champion*).

He is still shadow-boxing with his captured colleague when a policeman turns up; whereupon it all turns into a ballet. After which Charlie performs an acrobatic balancing act on the ladder while polishing the globes of the street lamps. Naturally, he falls off; but immediately makes sure his own watch is still ticking. A further struggle with his colleague is interrupted by the pawnbroker. Instantly they both put on an act of being harmlessly busy. But the pawnbroker sees through Charlie, and tells him he is

Chaplin analyzed this clock to complete destruction in a classic scene from *The Pawnbroker*, 1916. Albert Austin is the customer.

sacked. In a masterly manner Charlie mimes the starvation which, in that case, awaits a whole brood of children; the pawnbroker weakens, and Charlie is taken on again. Now he is beside himself with joy. As soon as the pawnbroker's back is turned, the two start fighting again.

The boss's daughter appears. Charlie arouses her sympathy by pretending to be hurt. He is invited into the kitchen. Here he places a long piece of dough round his neck like an Hawaiian garland, one moment using a ladle as a ukelele, the next swiping his colleague with the dough. The pawnbroker enters and Charlie —suddenly transformed into a baker—runs his lump of dough through a mangle.

The film's climax comes with Charlie behind the counter. The first client to appear is a theatrical old fellow, who is on the rocks and has to pawn a gold ring, his only valuable possession. Charlie is touched. Finding nothing less than a five dollar bill in the till, he hands it to him. Whereupon the old man, to Charlie's amazement, promptly gives him change!

After walking the tightrope of a piece of rope on the floor, pretending he is walking over an abyss—a trick which Chaplin varies in *The Circus*—he resumes his sweeping. At the same time the shop is being visited by a burglar. Taken by surprise by Edna, the burglar first pretends to pawn his umbrella and then announces his interest in buying up the whole shop. He is introduced to the boss, and Charlie has to attend to the next client—a man with an alarm clock.

Together with the bread scene in *The Gold Rush*, the long scene which follows, in which Charlie subjects the clock to such expert examination that he ultimately demolishes it, is perhaps the most famous of Chaplin's entire career. After examining the clock medically through a stethoscope he attacks it with a hammer and a drill, opens it up with a tin opener, sniffs suspiciously at the contents and scrutinises them through a watchmaker's glass. Then, with a pair of pliers he pulls out the entire works, springs and all, and as the mainspring begins dancing wildly about on the counter tries to oil them. Finally he sweeps the ruins of the alarm clock into the client's hat and hands it back to him with an apologetic shrug —it's simply not worth pawning...

Yet another bout of fisticuffs with his colleague follows, in which the pawnbroker and the burglar also become involved. In an unguarded moment the burglar, who has been admiring a collection of jewellery and is unaware that Charlie, fleeing from his boss's wrath, is hiding in a chest, breaks into the safe and plunders it. Just as he is threatening the pawnbroker and his employee with a pistol, Charlie pops out of the chest and hits him with a rolling pin. The fortune has been rescued. All is forgiven. The girl is Charlie's!

Chaplin's creative imagination celebrates real triumph in *The Pawnshop*. It contains samples of the entire range of his art, both in its humaner and less humane aspects. It was also the film in which Henry Bergman made his widely noted début with Chaplin. From now on he was to be his most faithful collaborator. The statement by a French author that Bergman had played extra roles in four earlier Mutual films seems dubious; it has been impossible to identify him in any of them.

In *Behind the Screen*, 1916, Chaplin
was again teamed up with Edna
Purviance and Eric Campbell as the
hapless foreman.

57   Behind the Screen (2 reel)

FIRST NIGHT 13 Nov 1916
MAIN FRENCH TITLE Charlot Fait du Ciné
DIRECTOR AND SCRIPTWRITER Charlie Chaplin
ACTORS Chaplin (scene-shifter in a film studio),
Edna Purviance (girl looking for a job in movies),
Eric Campbell (foreman of the scene-shifters), Albert Austin,
John Rand and Leo White (scene-shifters), Henry Bergman
(director of an historical film), Lloyd Bacon (director
of comedies), James T. Kelly (cameraman), Charlotte Mineau
and Leota Bryan (actresses), Wesley Ruggles and
Tom Wood (actors), Frank J. Coleman (producer)

96

The girl, Edna, is trying to find a job in films, but no one in the studio pays her the least attention. Charlie, working like a slave as a scene-shifter, is being ordered about by the foreman. As the former sits taking it easy in a chair, Charlie provides him with cushions and a spitoon. Three films are being shot simultaneously; one is historical, another is a drama on the edge of a trapdoor, and the third is a comedy which has reached the pie-chucking scene.

Charlie is in full form. Repeatedly he pulls over a camera, upsets a huge pillar and throws the shootings into chaos and at the same time carries Herculean loads—twelve chairs and a piano! He even manages *en passant* to trim a bearskin. At lunch Charlie reacts strongly to the smell of his neighbour's raw onions and tries to shelter from it by donning a knight's helmet, only opening the visor in order to take bites at his sandwich. Later he also takes surreptitious bites at his neighbour's chop, an idea taken from a similar scene in *His Trysting Place* (1914) and plagiarised long afterwards in *The Circus* with the episode with the little boy eating a sausage.

The scene-shifters' boss is not popular. After lunch is over the workers decide to go on strike. Only Charlie gets on with his job. But here come reinforcements—namely the girl. Seeing her chance, she puts on an overall and a cap.

During the shooting of one of the dramas Charlie is ordered to operate the lever of a trapdoor. Not only does the foreman vanish into the underworld—he also gets his head caught in it when he tries to come up again. (The Swedish censors reacted strongly against this!) After this the trapdoor is used for a number of unexpected disappearances.

Charlie realises that the 'boy' is a girl in disguise, falls for her charms and begins kissing her. When the foreman sees this he thinks they are a couple of homosexuals and acts accordingly. Foreman and Charlie go into action in a furious pie-chucking scene—a film within the film—which ends with Charlie taking cover behind a table. Although victorious, he has to strike his flag. *Behind the Screen*, incidentally, is the only Chaplin film to contain a *major* pie-throwing scene. I know of only two which are longer (though of course there may be more): namely, in Ben Turpin's *Keystone Hotel* (1935) and in Laurel and Hardy's almost legendary *The Battle of the Century* (1927). The end of *Behind the Screen* is devoted to the scene-shifters' dynamite coup, which causes widespread havoc in the studio. Charlie, of course, survives; so does Edna, his beloved.

This film, too, is a regression to the Keystone style. Although it has its subtle values, it is hardly one of the better films in the Mutual series. In 1918 it was totally banned in Sweden as 'brutalising', but there is a suggestion that the fictive 'homosexual' scenes were the really sensitive point. Nevertheless it was given an X certificate the following year, and passed for children in 1926.

58 The Rink (2 reel)

FIRST NIGHT 4 Dec 1916
MAIN FRENCH TITLE Charlot Patine
DIRECTOR AND SCRIPTWRITER Charlie Chaplin
ACTORS Chaplin (waiter, expert on roller skates),
Edna Purviance (a society girl), James T. Kelly (her father,
an ageing Don Juan), Eric Campbell (Mr Stout, Edna's
admirer), Henry Bergman (Mrs Stout; also an indignant
diner in the restaurant), Lloyd Bacon (a distinguished
guest), Albert Austin (chef and 'roller skater'),
Frank J. Coleman (manager of the restaurant),
John Rand (waiter), Charlotte Mineau and Leota Bryan
(friends of Edna's)

Chaplin is a waiter in a restaurant. So adept is he at his job that he writes out a bill from traces of the meal which the obese diner Mr Stout has left upon his person. In the swing doors to the kitchen Charlie collides with his fellow waiter, whose tray he upsets, and contrives to put a scrubbing brush, soap and a rag on one of his plates. Charlie next gives a brilliant demonstration of the art of mixing drinks. Whereupon chaos breaks loose in the restaurant.

Among the diners two newcomers discover they know each other well, namely Edna's father and Mr Stout's wife. Their amours lead to complications.

Charlie uses his lunch break for an excursion to the roller skating rink, where Edna and Mr Stout also turn up. The former becomes the object of the latter's attentions, as intensive as they are unwelcome. But when Charlie performs on the rink, attitudes change: his giddy skating act entirely takes the wind out of Mr Stout's sail. This sequence, a ballet-like composition in which at times Edna is the third party, contains samples of Chaplin's virtuosity and equilibristic gifts.

Charlie and Edna elude the infuriated Mr Stout, and Charlie, presenting himself as Sir Cecil Seltzer, is invited by Edna to a roller-skating party. Here all parties meet up. Edna's daddy has invited Mrs Stout, and Mr Stout is in the company of another lady (Charlotte Mineau). Under Charlie's leadership their painful encounter soon turns into a frantic dance.

His new roller-skating duel with Mr Stout and his dance with Mrs Stout form the climax of a party which ends with the police being called in and the assembled company driving Charlie out into the street. He escapes on roller skates, caught up on a car.

Like most of the other Mutual comedies, *The Rink* has been revived innumerable times, both on its own and in cavalcades. Even today it has lost nothing of its stylishness or impact.

59 Easy Street (2 reel)

FIRST NIGHT 22 Jan 1917
MAIN FRENCH TITLE Charlot Policeman
DIRECTOR AND SCRIPTWRITER Charlie Chaplin
ACTORS Chaplin (a vagabond), Edna Purviance (girl
working at a missionary station), Albert Austin (clergyman;
also a policeman), Eric Campbell (the terror of the
streets), Henry Bergman (an anarchist who makes off
with Charlie), Loyal Underwood (father of a poor and
numerous brood of children; also a policeman),
Charlotte Mineau (an ungrateful woman), Tom Wood
(chief of police), Lloyd Bacon (drug addict), Leota Bryan
(mother of the children), Frank J. Coleman
(policeman), Janet Miller Sully and John Rand
(visitors to the mission)

Lured by the hymn-singing, Charlie the tramp enters a mission and sits down among the congregation. For a while he takes his neighbour's baby on his knee, but when the infant pees on him regrets it. He manages to get hold of the collection box; but on meeting Edna, the beautiful missionary sister, is stricken with remorse.

Meanwhile a shindy has broken out on Easy Street, where the town bully and his henchmen are running amuck. The police are powerless. Anyone venturing into the thick of the fray is carried off on a stretcher. But Charlie knows nothing of all this. Happening to pass the police station he sees a notice appealing for recruits. Softened up by the missionaries he applies for a job, gets it, and exchanges his bowler for a helmet.

At once Charlie is put on the beat on Easy Street, the street being tyrannised by the bully. Their encounter is dramatic. Charlie tries out his truncheon on the big fellow's head without the least

Charlie was a vagabond turned policeman in *Easy Street*, 1917.

result; whereupon the latter, to show off his strength, bends a
lamp-post double. As he does so Charlie leaps on to him, gets his
head into the casing of the lamp, and turns on the gas. The giant
collapses. Police are summoned, and the tyrant is carried off to the
lockup. Charlie is the hero of the day. He helps a poor woman by
giving her groceries which he pinches from a street stall, but all the
thanks he gets is a flowerpot on his head. After this he helps Edna
take presents to a family with many children. Astounded, he con-
gratulates the diminutive father on his prowess.

Meanwhile the bully has broken out of gaol and is causing may-
hem in his own home. Charlie, summoned by his wife, is chased
round the town and back again into the bully's home, from which

100

he has to escape through the window, only to find his antagonist waiting for him outside. Again Charlie runs inside and chucks an iron stove out of the window, knocking his adversary out a second time.

Edna, who has attempted to intervene, is kidnapped. A sinister character takes her down into a cellar where a drug addict has his lair. Charlie, too, has been attacked by the bully's henchmen and is flung into the same room. After another battle with the scum of the streets he rescues Edna and breaks out.

Peace is restored on Easy Street. People have learned to respect Charlie, and the bully too has been converted by the missionaries. With Edna on his arm Constable Charlie takes a promenade. Once again he is enjoying the blessings of the mission.

Easy Street is Chaplin's most famous and popular two-reeler, a

Eric Campbell was the local bully in *East Street*, 1917.

story whose social satire, which he was to develop so strongly in his later films, is easily discerned. Here we have the prototype of the little fellow who successfully takes up the struggle with the big guys. But his fight is fought with hard knocks, and when the Swedish censors first (1918) saw the film they blacklisted it with their standard 'brutalising'. Later that year, however, *Easy Street* was passed for adult audiences. It was not until 1935 that Swedish children were admitted to *Easy Street*.

60 The Cure (2 reel)

FIRST NIGHT 16 Apl 1917
MAIN FRENCH TITLE Charlot Fait une Cure
DIRECTOR AND SCRIPTWRITER Charlie Chaplin
ACTORS Chaplin (visitor at a health spa), Edna Purviance
(young girl), Eric Campbell (gouty gentleman),
Henry Bergman (masseur), Albert Austin (tall male nurse),
John Rand (male nurse and second masseur), James T. Kelly
(piccolo with beard), Frank J. Coleman (spa director),
Leota Bryan (nurse), Tom Wood (patient who has
shoes flung at his head), Janet Miller Sully and
Loyal Underwood (visitors taking the waters)

Defying notices banning all alcohol Charlie arrives at a spa. His big trunk turns out to contain a stock of strong liquors. For once he

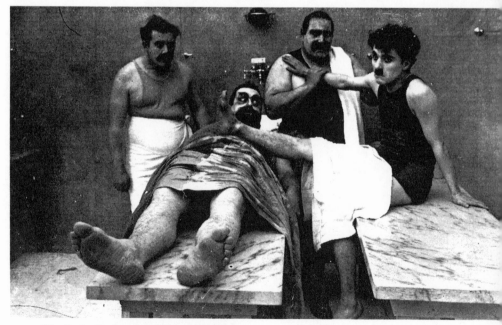

Charlie in the hands of Henry Bergman as the masseur in *The Cure*, 1917. On the next table is his perennial nemesis, Eric Campbell.

is wearing a straw hat and a light blazer. At his very first contact with the spa's clientèle he is already tight. In one of the establishment's swing doors, he collides with a heavily-built visitor with a bandaged foot (Eric Campbell). So urgent is his desire to force an entrance that the latter's foot and Charlie's head both somehow contrive to get badly squeezed, thus instantly precipitating hostilities. The scene is made to yield more comedy than can readily be imagined.

Invited to drink the waters, Charlie objects to their taste. In his own person the spa attendant demonstrates what superb muscles one can get from taking the cure, whereupon Charlie checks up by examining the biceps of a pretty neighbour. Spilling his cup, he accuses a toy dog of having caused the puddle.

Instead of drinking the health-giving waters, he devotes himself to his own stock of liquor up in his room. Then it is time for the first encounter with the beautiful Edna. Down in the foyer, her husband—the man with the bandaged foot—is in fond attendance upon her. Charlie misunderstands the state of affairs and contrives to remove a chair from beneath the eminent guest, who summons the spa director. The latter wishes to eject Charlie; but Edna intervenes, saying the incident was due to her husband's clumsiness.

The next scene takes us to the massage and bath department. Ordered to undress, Charlie tosses his shoes over the curtain and precipitates a quarrel between his antagonist and another patient.

Charlie's bathing is highly idiosyncratic. He dips his foot in the swimming pool and then makes swimming motions on the edge of the bath. Now he must undergo massage. Horrified at the stupid masseur's rough treatment of another patient, he proclaims him the winner. Now it is his own turn. Slipping repeatedly out of the masseur's grasp, he flees to the sauna where he mimes a wrestling match. In the end the masseur capitulates and the gouty gentleman tumbles into the pool.

Meanwhile some of the staff are dipping into Charlie's liquor store. The spa director discovers them and orders them to throw the stuff away. The bottles fly out of the window into the pool, whose waters instantly acquire unprecedented strength and flavour.

The entire establishment now begins to loosen up. In the general frenzy Edna, chased by inebriated guests, is saved by Charlie. She prevails upon him to try out the salubrious effects of the spa waters. Reluctantly he does so; but one mouthful suffices to convert him. Pouring it down his throat by the jugful he gets so thoroughly tight that he frightens away the fair object of his affections. Once again, he runs into his antagonist and gives his wheelchair such a shove that the invalid tumbles head first into the pool. Next day we see a chastened Charlie with an ice-bag under his hat. Reconciled to Edna, he goes with her to take the waters. Naturally, Charlie contrives to fall in.

61   The Immigrant (2 reel)

FIRST NIGHT 17 June 1917
MAIN FRENCH TITLE L'Émigrant
DIRECTOR AND SCRIPTWRITER Charlie Chaplin
ACTORS Chaplin (an emigrant), Edna Purviance
(girl emigrant), Kitty Bradbury (her mother), Albert Austin
(a Russian emigrant prone to seasickness; later, a diner

in a restaurant, Charlie's neighbour), Henry Bergman
(the big lady on the boat; later, the artist in the
restaurant), Eric Campbell (waiter), Stanley Sanford
(chief gambler on board), James T. Kelly (shabby
character in the restaurant), John Rand (restaurant guest
who is broke and gets badly mauled), Frank J. Coleman
(the restaurant owner; also one of the ship's officers),
Loyal Underwood (emigrant)

Aboard an emigrant ship Charlie is on his way to the USA, the
land of his dreams. When we first encounter him he is leaning over
the ship's rail, apparently in the worst throes of seasickness. To our
surprise we see he is in fact fishing, as he pulls up a fish. Another
passenger who is smitten with seasickness on the violently rolling
vessel makes Charlie sick, too. But this does not stop him from
joining in the race to the dinner table. In the shabby saloon both
diners and dishes skid to and fro. When the pretty Edna comes in,
Charlie chivalrously gives up his seat to her and goes out to join a
nasty-looking gang of gamblers on deck. He wins, but is only
allowed to keep his money after a furious tussle involving an axe
and a pistol.

At that moment Edna discovers to her terror that her sick mother
has been robbed in her sleep of all the money they possess for their
journey. Charlie comes to the weeping Edna's rescue, and when she
is not looking stuffs the money he has just won into her bag.
Deciding on second thoughts to keep something for himself he is
just taking back a single bank note when the purser spots him, and
of course accuses him of being the thief. The episode is sorted out
by the grateful Edna.

Now America is approaching. The Statue of Liberty appears at
the exact moment when the passengers are being roped in like a
flock of sheep prior to their confrontation with immigration officials. Charlie casts a second and more suspicious glance at the
Statue of Liberty.

Time passes. Now we are in New York. As Charlie, broke and
hungry, passes a restaurant he chances to see a silver coin lying on
the street. Picking it up he walks gaily into the restaurant. There
he infuriates a loud-voiced and powerfully-built waiter by insisting
on keeping his hat on. Nevertheless he is served a portion of beans,
which he threads one by one on to his fork. At that moment he
notices Edna. She is sitting at another table, wearing black mourn-
ing gloves. Her mother has died. Charlie puts his arm round her,
invites her over to his table and orders a second portion.

In *The Immigrant*, 1917, with Edna
Purviance and Kitty Bradbury, as her
mother.

Nearby, a drama is going on. A guest cannot pay his bill. Charlie,
horrified, watches him being beaten up by six of the male personnel before being flung out. He was ten cents short, remarks the
waiter coldly.

Instinctively, Charlie puts his hand into his pocket—and goes
stiff with terror. His coin has gone! There is a hole in his pocket.
To put as bold a face on it as possible and play for time he orders
Edna a cup of coffee, but prepares for the worst. However, a hobo
who has picked up his coin has just sat down beside him. After the
tramp has paid the waiter, the coin again drops to the floor. Charlie
tries to put his foot on it; but the waiter, suspicious and unaware
that he himself is standing on it, searches about him for the coin—
the object on which the whole sequence hinges.

In the end it is Charlie who gets hold of it. But when he wants to pay, the waiter declares it counterfeit and refuses to accept it. Another cup of coffee to gain time. And now here comes someone who is to save the situation—an artist. Instantly fascinated by Edna's possibilities as a model, he moves over to their table. When the waiter comes over again and threatens Charlie with his bill, the artist offers to pay. For appearances' sake Charlie declares he would not dream of such a thing. The artist insists. Again Charlie declines—once too often. The artist lets him pay for himself.

So Charlie is as badly off as ever. But fortunately the artist, after paying his own bill, has laid a generous tip on the plate. Charlie just has time to snap it up and pay his, and the waiter curses artists for their stinginess.

Eric Campbell is the waiter in this scene from *The Immigrant,* 1917. With Chaplin and Edna Purviance is Henry Bergman, as an artist who rescues the hapless couple.

Now Charlie and Edna are out in the street. A time is fixed for Edna to pose, and Charlie manages to extract a few dollars' advance, enough for a marriage licence. Proudly, Charlie drags off his happy if recalcitrant Edna to find the nearest clergyman.

In the first act of *The Immigrant*, as in *Easy Street*, one can distinguish an element of social satire alongside the farce. America, for those who emigrated to it around the turn of the century, was hardly the dreamland they had imagined. If Charlie had known then what he knew forty years later he would have cast more than one suspicious glance up at the Statue of Liberty. Probably he would have introduced a whole scene of intense indignation. An instance of the care devoted by Chaplin to his Mutual films is *The Immigrant's* original footage, some 40,000ft (more than usual for a full-length feature film). It was edited to 2,067ft.

62   The Adventurer (2 reel)

FIRST NIGHT 23 Oct 1917
MAIN FRENCH TITLE Charlot s'Évade
DIRECTOR AND SCRIPTWRITER Charlie Chaplin
ACTORS Chaplin (gaolbird on the run), Edna Purviance
(family girl), Henry Bergman (her father; also a docker who
can swim), Marta Golden (her mother), Eric Campbell
(her suitor), Albert Austin (butler), Kono (family chauffeur),
John Rand (guest), Frank J. Coleman (fat warder on the
shore), Loyal Underwood (little bearded guest), May White
(plump lady who gets an ice-cream down her neck),
Phyllis Allen (housemaid)

Charlie has escaped from Sing-Sing. A notice tells us that a prize of $1,000 has been placed on his head—the first head to pop up in the film, out of the sandy beach near Santa Monica, where the film was shot. Having burrowed his way up out of the sand, Charlie finds he is staring straight into the muzzle of a gun belonging to a warder, who is taking a rest. Digging himself in again, Charlie waits until the warder dozes off, and then leaves his hideout.

The warder, suddenly wide awake, tumbles into the hole Charlie has left behind him; and at once the chase is up. Charlie, wearing his prison clothes, simply 'runs' up the face of the cliffs (a most effective piece of trick-filming). Reaching the summit he mocks the warder who is still down on the road.

Unfortunately, the law has a second representative up on the heights. Charlie however, by means of a series of acrobatic stunts in a lying position, manages to elude his grasp and kicks his second pursuer over the edge. Still on the run, he tricks a third warder into thinking he has shot him down. 'Playing dead', he kicks him too over the precipice. Finally, with the help of a gun cunningly filched from the enemy, he overcomes a quartet of pursuers and swims out to sea; steals the bathing costume of a yachtsman who is taking a dip and when the warders' boat capsizes in the breakers, escapes.

Inside a nearby villa dramatic events are afoot. The daughter of the house (Edna) is being courted by 'the strong man', who is showing off his strength to her. But when Edna's mother is threatened by drowning he has not the courage to jump from the jetty and save her. So Edna jumps instead. Her suitor, too, ends up in the water, owing to the presence of a massive docker who crushes the jetty's rail and as he falls drags the coward after him.

Charlie, still swimming, has approached the scene of the drama. He is just in time to rescue Edna and then—more dubiously—her less appetising mother. But when he goes so far in playing the good Samaritan as to include her suitor in his rescue operations the latter brutally tramples him under water. Unconscious, Charlie floats ashore and is found underneath the pier by the family's faithful chauffeur. The two ladies take him back to their comfortable home. There he can rest and reap his laurels.

In *The Adventurer*, 1917, Albert
Austin appeared with Chaplin.

Morning. Charlie wakes up in an unknown bedroom. His striped pyjamas, lent him by his friends, remind him of prison; likewise the bars of his bedstead. But the footman brings him worthier raiment and by evening he is ready to participate in a family banquet. He makes short work of the liquor, adeptly switching his neighbour's full glass with his own empty one. Edna, to her massive suitor's annoyance, is much impressed by Charlie's attentions. But the suitor finds he has a trump card. Out on the verandah his eye falls on a newspaper. On the first page is Charlie's 'wanted' face. He reports the matter to Edna's father. Meanwhile Charlie, guessing there is something in the wind, has seen the photo and corrected its features to cast suspicion on his rival.

Now a greater danger arises. One of the warders has wormed his way into the cook's good graces. Charlie falls into such a panic that even the popping of a champagne cork is enough to make him throw up his hands. While Charlie is dancing, his rival rings up the prison and reports the fugitive. But before the long arm of the law finally catches up with him, Charlie has time for an ice-cream with Edna on the balcony and drops his ice down his hostess's back. A gentleman friend who helpfully searches for it in her décolletage has his face slapped for his pains.

And so the time has come for the hectic finale. The warders march in and Charlie achieves miracles of escapism, for example, by pretending to be a lampstand. He teaches his rival another lesson, kisses the beautiful Edna and formally presents her to the warder who has discovered them in an embrace. The ensuing handshakes give Charlie the necessary breathing-space to leave the scene for good.

The family chauffeur is none other than the Japanese Kono, Chaplin's own private chauffeur and factotum. From 1916 until 1934 Kono served him both as butler, chauffeur, secretary, masseur and bodyguard—an admirable and taciturn person.

The Adventurer forms a worthy close to Chaplin's Mutual films. It contains innumerable examples of his capacity for inventing gags. Rarely has he more elegantly demonstrated his grace, his nimbleness and his imagination. It is a passing-out exam before facing greater tasks yet to come.

The First National Period

Already in the new year 1917–18 Chaplin was in full swing working on his first film for First National (afterwards absorbed into Warner Brothers). Apart from *Tillie's Punctured Romance*, this was his longest film hitherto, and the one which was to establish Chaplin's reputation as a satirist. He called it *A Dog's Life*.

His new contract, which staggered the entire movie world, guaranteed him one million dollars for eight films over an eighteen-month period, plus a $15,000 bonus on signing the contract. Under it, Chaplin was to stand all production costs. He built his own studio on La Brea Avenue in what is now down-town Hollywood. There all his future American films were to be made.

Chaplin fulfilled his contract, but not within the specified time. Five years were to pass before his new series was complete; but it was to include one long film, one four-reeler and three three-reelers. This still further augmented his fee, which had been based on two-reelers.

Chaplin retained a good many of the actors from his Mutual ensemble. Unfortunately, one of his main supports, the gigantic Eric Campbell, had died in a car accident in December 1917. But Edna Purviance, Henry Bergman, Albert Austin and John Rand were among those who remained faithful. He also received an admirable reinforcement in his half-brother, Sydney Chaplin, who had already established an independent reputation for himself as a film comedian. Another valuable newcomer was Chuck Riesner, who was both an actor and Chaplin's assistant director. All the First National films were shot by Rollie Totheroh—who by this time had come to 'know' his Chaplin thoroughly.

First National gave Chaplin almost limitlessly free hands and the necessary peace of mind to develop his vagabond figure in a more serious and realistic context, pointed up with typically Chaplinesque satire and finely calculated gags.

Except insofar as his private life came to exert a direct influence on his film work—as was the case when completing *The Circus*—

the disturbance of Chaplin's peace of mind which arose from a series of marital problems, beginning in 1918 with Mildred Harris, does not concern us here. The major problems of his love-life were not to occur until later.

63 A Dog's Life (3 reel)

FIRST NIGHT 14 Apl 1918
MAIN FRENCH TITLE Une Vie de Chien
DIRECTOR AND SCRIPTWRITER Charlie Chaplin
ACTORS Chaplin (tramp), Edna Purviance (girl who sings and dances in the café), Tom Wilson (policeman), Sydney Chaplin (owner of the lunch stall), Albert Austin (tall thin villain), Henry Bergman (big drunken fellow who is looking for a job; also a woman guest in the dance hall), Chuck Riesner (employee in an employment office; also the drummer), Billy White (owner of the café), Bud Jamison (the strong villain), James T. Kelly, Park Jones, Janet Miller Sully, Loyal Underwood

Charlie the tramp has fixed himself up a provisional dwelling in the remains of a yard next to a draughty paling, everywhere pierced with cracks and openings. When an itinerant hot dog man chances to take up his stand on the other side of the paling, Charlie sniffs in the scent of his hot dogs the chance of a free meal. Through a hole he manages to filch both a sausage and some mustard but, realising a policeman's eyes are on him, he quickly puts them back again. The policeman goes to the attack. But Charlie, by rolling himself to and fro under the palings, always manages to be on the safe side and despite police reinforcements contrives to escape.

When strolling in the town he notices an employment agency is offering a job in a brewery. He rushes in, but finds he has many competitors. All are waiting on a bench until such time as the counter clerks shall open the two little shutters. The question is, which to choose? Always Charlie makes the wrong choice; always there is another man ahead of him. In vain he rushes from one shutter to the other, and when at long last he reaches the head of the queue all the others have got jobs and no more are to be had. This perfectly timed scene immortally instances an all too common experience.

In his 'kennel', a washtub in the vicinity of Charlie's camp, another outcast is waking up: a bitch called Scraps. She goes out into the street to look for something edible but when at long last she finds it, is attacked by other strays. Charlie, watching the fight, succeeds in rescuing Scraps, and then flees, after sending the pack of stray dogs scrambling over a grocery stall. One of them rips a strip from the seat of his trousers before he and his new-found friend reach safety.

They end up in front of a lunch stall. Charlie and Scraps, moving like lightning, manage to empty a whole plate of cakes and in spite of the stallkeeper's (Sydney Chaplin) hawklike glances, supply themselves with sausages. Again the policeman appears and they have to beat a retreat.

In a nearby shabby dance hall Edna who, shy and reluctant, has a job as a singer and dancing girl, is being forced by the manager to associate with his mixed clientèle. Charlie, with Scraps hidden away in his spacious back pocket, enters the hall where he draws a certain amount of attention—the dog's wagging tail is sticking out through a hole in his trousers. The drummer of the band is confused by the tail, which begins beating out rolls on his drum.

Though Edna's singing moves her audience to tears, the boss is displeased by her reluctance to associate with his clients, and threatens to fire her. Charlie takes her under his wing and gives a demonstration dance, a dance complicated by the need to hang on to Scraps's lead. As soon as the management realises that Charlie cannot pay for his meal he is chucked out.

In the town a tipsy gentleman has been robbed by two sinister characters. With the police at their heels they have found it advisable to hide his wallet by burying it on the very spot where Charlie has his 'home'. Charlie and his faithful Scraps come home to rest. Scraps digs up the wallet, which Charlie finds is stuffed with banknotes.

Charlie and the dog return to the dance hall for a merry evening. He finds Edna sitting on a bench. She has just been given the sack. Immediately he begins planning a future for them on a country farm, but the two robbers, chancing to overhear their conversation, attack Charlie and take back the wallet. Once again, for lack of cash, Charlie is chucked out. But he recovers and returns to take his revenge.

In a sketch whose design can only be called a work of genius, he knocks out one of the two thieves at the same time as, from behind a curtain, he manages to continue a 'conversation' with gestures—a fantastic piece of pantomime. The upshot is that thief number two is disposed of also. Once again the wallet changes owner. After an uproar in the dance hall Charlie, the thieves at his heels, flees. He seeks shelter from their pot-shots behind the counter of the unfortunate owner of the lunch stall. In the end Charlie is overwhelmed, but the faithful Scraps successfully rescues the wallet. The police intervene and peace is restored.

The epilogue shows us Charlie, now a proud owner of a farm, working out in the fields; and thereafter a homely idyll, in which he and Edna, married, are exchanging loving glances over a layette. In it lies Scraps, with a litter of puppies.

Like *The Kid*, *A Dog's Life* unquestionably bears Chaplin's authentic signature. Its story, set against a background of wretched social conditions, is worked up into a real drama. The narrative, at once charming and bitterly satirical, has many farcical episodes of surprising ingenuity. All the while one feels it is firmly rooted in the social realities of those days.

64 The Bond (split reel)

Charlie Chaplin in a Liberty Bond Appeal was made in 1918 in aid of The Liberty Loan Committee as part of the effort to back up the American war effort. For details see chapter on Chaplin's 'unknown' films.

65 Shoulder Arms (3 reel)

FIRST NIGHT 20 Nov 1918
FRENCH TITLE Charlot Soldat
DIRECTOR AND SCRIPTWRITER Charlie Chaplin
ACTORS Chaplin (a recruit and 'dream soldier'), Edna Purviance (French girl), Sydney Chaplin (American sergeant; also the Kaiser), Jack Wilson (German Crown Prince), Henry Bergman (fat German sergeant; also the bar tender; Field Marshal von Hindenburg), Albert Austin (American officer; also German soldier; the Kaiser's chauffeur), Tom Wilson (sergeant in the American camp), John Rand (American soldier), Park Jones, Loyal Underwood

It is World War I, Charlie has been called up and is in an American training camp. Drilled by a grim sergeant he does his best, but like the good soldier Schweik mostly does the exact opposite of what is required. His feet are giving him trouble, and he has some difficulty in knowing right from left.

Charlie as a raw recruit in *Shoulder Arms*, 1918.

On guard duty in *Shoulder Arms*, 1918.

Now we are on the Western Front. In an American sector of the trenches Charlie, staggering under an immense load of equipment which includes a little mousetrap—of course the sergeant's finger gets caught in it—arrives in the theatre of war. Settled into his dug-out, Charlie immediately hangs up a cheese-grater on the wall to alleviate his itching back.

But soon Charlie has more things to worry about than lice. Out in the pouring rain and with his helmet shaking under a torrent of shells, he mounts guard. During his turn of guard duty he dreams of Broadway and of a bar (parallel scenes in divided frames, an advanced technique for 1918).

The post arrives from home. It brings letters and parcels for everyone—except Charlie. Depressed, he declines his comrades' offer of a sandwich—the bait from his mousetrap will do for him. In an unforgettable scene Charlie, reading one of his comrades' letters over his shoulder, mirrors his facial expressions as he reacts to its varied contents.

Glimpses from the nearby German trench show a surly little officer mustering his tall men. Charlie is about to encounter the foe for the first time. Finally he too receives a parcel which, alas only contains a carton of dog biscuits and an evil-smelling Gorgonzola cheese. Horrified. Charlie puts on his gasmask and lobs the cheese like a hand-grenade over to the enemy lines, where it lands in the officer's face.

Down in the dugout, half-filled now with rainwater, Charlie passes a restless night, bedding down under the surface with his pillow and blanket; and so does the sergeant. A frog seats itself on his foot. Charlie brings a flaming light—it is not too clear where it has come from—to bear on the sergeant's feet, and reaches its target. In the morning Charlie massages his feet which are frozen stiff dredging a large foot—the sergeant's—and a small one—his own—out of the depths.

Now it is nearly zero hour. Charlie together with the others is making ready to 'go over the top'. The omens do not seem propitious. His identity disc bears the number thirteen and he manages to smash his pocket mirror into a thousand pieces. But in the end he reaches the top of the storming ladder, and in the next scene returns triumphant, having captured thirteen of the foe single-handed. Asked how he contrived to do it he gives the classic answer: 'I surrounded them.'

A meal break in the trench with the sergeant offers some genuine Chaplinesque gags. He uncorks his bottle with the aid of an enemy bullet, lights his cigarette with another, performs miracles as a sniper and even shoots down an enemy aircraft.

116

But new exploits are still to come. Volunteers are called for, and Charlie steps forward—only to withdraw briskly when he hears the task is a perilous one. But there is no getting out of it. Charlie takes all due precautions by appearing in the enemy lines disguised as a tree.

A German unit has been ordered to cut down trees. Charlie, close to being felled at the root, succeeds in knocking down the whole gang, only to be faced with new trials when another unit appears with his friend the sergeant. They have taken him prisoner. After saving him from the firing squad, Charlie is chased by the German sergeant into a wood. There, after a dramatic game of hide-and-seek, he is again saved by his disguise. The chase ends in a drain, where the fat German gets stuck.

Exhausted, Charlie seeks repose in the burnt out ruins of a house. Here his delightful slumbers are interrupted by a young French girl—the only survivor. In mime Charlie tries to explain he is an American soldier—knocks his own head and draws the star-spangled banner in the air. This fond scene is terminated by the arrival of German soldiers. Charlie escapes by the skin of his teeth. But the girl is seized for having sheltered an enemy soldier, and taken away to headquarters. She is interrogated by an officer, who makes indecent approaches to her. Charlie comes down the chimney and beats him up, and hides him away in a cupboard.

Sensation—the kaiser, the crown prince and Field Marshal von Hindenburg are all arriving on a tour of inspection. Before the dignitaries Charlie, dressed up in his defeated enemy's uniform, brilliantly takes off the manner of a German officer. After which he rescues his friend the sergeant a second time.

Luring the kaiser's staff away from his car Charlie knocks them out and takes the place of the chauffeur. The girl, disguised by a moustache, becomes the kaiser's new escort. Now the tour of inspection is over. The kaiser and the crown prince drive off—right through the allied lines. Charlie is the hero of the hour, and in the general excitement takes his chance to give the kaiser a kick in the pants. Now we are in New York, with an autocade in Charlie's honour passing down Broadway. A statue of Charlie, the size of the Statue of Liberty, can be seen. But it is only in his dreams. Charlie, still the recruit, is rudely awakened in his tent and turns out once more to drill.

Originally *Shoulder Arms* was to have been a five-reeler, but it was cut down to three to give it a firmer rhythm. Among the scenes which were cut is the one in which Charlie is praised by President Poincaré, and King George snips off one of his buttons as a souvenir. Reflecting on the matter Chaplin decided not to carry a joke too far.

The film had its first night only three weeks before the Armistice. Many were afraid its subject would be too sensitive and feared for its reception. But this was everywhere overwhelmingly favourable. Personally I regard *Shoulder Arms* as one of the priceless gems in Chaplin's collection. Though his satire bites on the sheer absurdity and meaninglessness of war, he also depicts the comradeship of the rank and file. The setting, too, is realistic.

Unfortunately *Shoulder Arms* is another film which has been much messed about. As late as 1970 a drastically cut copy was imported into Sweden from Germany. Obviously the exporter had objected to fun being made of Germans. One of the scenes cut is the one in which the German lieutenant gets the cheese in his face. Another is the one in which Charlie puts him across his knee and gives him a caning.

66 Sunnyside (3 reel)

FIRST NIGHT 15 June 1919
FRENCH TITLE Une Idylle aux Champs
DIRECTOR AND SCRIPTWRITER Charlie Chaplin
ACTORS Chaplin (odd job man), Edna Purviance (local
beauty), Tom Wilson (head of the household), Tom Terris
(young man from the big city), Henry Bergman
(peasant, probably also Edna's father), Park Jones (fat man),
Loyal Underwood (little old man), Tom Wood (farmer).
A statement that Albert Austin plays in this film has
proved impossible to substantiate.

Charlie is odd-job man and factotum at the Evergreen Hotel—also on a farm—in the idyllic little town of Sunnyside, at the turn of the century. He has plenty to do. Under a hard employer he has to get up at 4am and goes late to bed. If it were not for his love for the beautiful Edna, the neighbour's daughter, life would not be worth living.

As the film begins, the farmer is making repeated but vain efforts to awaken the drowsy Charlie, who does not want to get up. Not to be taken by surprise he sleeps with his clothes on. At breakfast he gains time by bringing a cow into the house to supply cream direct for his coffee and a hen who lays an egg in the frying pan.

The highlight of the forenoon is his visit to Edna while her

118

harsh father has gone out. At Edna's no one is about except an imbecile farm hand, whom Charlie entices out of the way by pretending to play hide-and-seek with him. He causes him to run out into the street, where he almost gets run over. Charlie has plucked Edna a bouquet of flowers from her own garden, and also honours her with a ring. Some romantic music at the piano is interrupted first by a goat, which eats up important pages in the music, and then by Edna's father, who causes Charlie to beat a hasty retreat.

While his master is busying himself with church matters, Charlie drives the cows out to graze. At the same time he is so deeply absorbed in reading that he does not notice the cows have wandered off into a side road. When he gives a pair of broad haunches a crack with his stick he finds they do not belong to a cow but to an indignant peasant woman.

In vain Charlie hunts about for his cows, which have found their way into town and into the church, where they are terrifying the congregation out of its wits. His attempts to drive the beasts out again only lead to his being tossed by the fiercest of them. He lands on her back and, after a perilous journey, is flung into a ditch.

Knocked senseless in his fall, Charlie dreams he is in the fields of Arcady, where four nymphs awaken him and lure him into the dance—a classical style ballet, spiced with Chaplinesque leaps and gestures. This pastoral idyll is interrupted when Charlie falls on a cactus and has to pluck out the prickles as he goes on dancing. He is aroused brusquely to the real state of affairs when some peasants out for a walk drag him up out of the ditch. After which, with a kick in the pants, he is sent off home to his furious employer.

A stranger has arrived in town. After a crash in his car outside the hotel he is carried in unconscious. By now Charlie has been promoted to hall porter. He tries to get the young man, who is in a dead faint, to write his name in the guest book. A homespun doctor is summoned and the patient undergoes a comic joint examination by him and by Charlie. The hotel's new guests having been duly attended to, a scene follows with Charlie cleaning up in the foyer, manoeuvring his mop among the irritated guests.

The man from the big city soon recovers and his sophisticated manners fascinate Edna, who instantly forgets all about her former admirer, Charlie. One funny detail is when Charlie tries to show his savoir-vivre by kissing Edna's hand. Unfortunately she has got some glue on it, and Charlie has difficulty in extricating himself from his kiss. The young man, too, has fallen for Edna, and sweeps her off her feet. Next time Charlie brings her a bouquet he finds his place is already occupied.

Obviously the best thing he can do is to try and resemble the snob. Pulling a sock over his shoe to imitate his spats, he conceals a light in the knob of his cane to compete with his rival's similarly situated cigarette lighter. All to no avail. Edna finds him absurd and gives him back his ring. Charlie, a broken man, vainly attempts to commit suicide by getting in the way of a car.

But the situation clears up. Soon the young man has wearied of small-town life and his flirtation with Edna. He is preparing to leave. Charlie rejoices: and Edna is furious. But as soon as her light of love has gone for good she takes Charlie back into her good graces and all is once again peace and harmony.

In its own day *Sunnyside* was regarded as a semi-failure. This is a questionable view. Among Chaplin's longer films it is something of an exception. Though it has certain typically Chaplinesque episodes, the poetry and rustic milieu dominate over the comedy. *Sunnyside* has its own special charm. It also contains one of Chaplin's finest dream sequences, the Arcadian ballet, with Charlie's dance among the nymphs. To place a farce in a rustic environment was also a novelty, and the idea was taken up by other comedians, notably Buster Keaton in *Go West*.

67   A Day's Pleasure (2 reel)

FIRST NIGHT 7 Dec 1919
ALTERNATIVE TITLE A Pleasant Day
FRENCH TITLE Une Journée de Plaisir
DIRECTOR AND SCRIPTWRITER Charlie Chaplin
ACTORS Chaplin (father), Edna Purviance (mother),
Jackie Coogan (their youngest son), Tom Wilson (married
man), Babe London (his seasick wife), Henry Bergman
(captain; also a gentleman in a car), Loyal Underwood (little
protesting gentleman on the street)

Charlie and his family are to make a Sunday excursion, and Charlie has difficulty starting up his old model-T Ford. As soon as he has got it going with the starting handle and is about to clamber in, the engine stops; only to start again on its own accord when he climbs out to see to it. But in the end the family set off. They board a coastal steamer. Even before the voyage begins they are involved in a couple of contretemps. Charlie runs off to buy some cigarettes. Whereupon a middle-aged couple come and squeeze themselves into his place; when Charlie comes back he has to wedge himself in again. Then, just as the captain is giving orders for the vessel to put to sea, a fat mother with a pram comes rushing down to the gangway, which is already being pulled in. The pram gets across but the mother is left dangling between the boat and the quay. Charlie, whose errand has taken him ashore, uses her as a bridge. After which she is dragged in over the ship's rail with a boathook.

The ship's negro band strikes up. Though there is a fair swell running, everyone joins in the dancing, staggering from one rail to the other, sometimes finding they are with the wrong partner. Charlie ends up beside the trombonist, who pale and seasick, pathetically begins filing away at Charlie's nose with his instrument and finally loses it overboard. A deck chair, after Charlie has demonstrated every thinkable way of *not* making it function, follows it.

Now the husband has gone to fetch his seasick better half a glass of water. Charlie, who is not feeling too good either, collapses on the bench beside the wife, his head droops and falls on to her massive lap. Whereupon the purser covers them both over with a rug. When the husband returns and sits down he gets a nasty shock when he finds he is not holding his wife's hand but Charlie's. In the ensuing commotion Charlie first gets the worst of it; but even the husband succumbs to bouts of seasickness and Charlie, plucking up courage, shows off his prowess as a boxer in the same magnificent manner as in *The Champion*. One moment both combatants are in high form; the next they are overwhelmed with seasickness. At long last the traumatic voyage comes to an end, and the passengers stagger ashore.

Now Charlie is on his way home with his children and some flowers in the model-T. But before it reaches its goal the car becomes the hub of a complicated traffic jam at a street junction, colliding with and upsetting a tar truck. Charlie and a policeman, each stuck as fast in the tar as the other, exchange furious words. Finally Charlie finds a solution to the problem, and his family can come home from *A Day's Pleasure*. This two-reeler was not kindly received by the contemporary press, perhaps because it was a regression to the Mutual epoch or even earlier. Yet *A Day's Pleasure* contains many delightful points and in my view ranks with a mediocre Mutual. Chaplin experts have generally preferred to place the traffic episode in its first act (before the embarkation). But contemporary press clippings tell us its proper place is at the end. The accident sequence provides a finale and a climax for the film as a whole.

68   The Kid (6 reel)

FIRST NIGHT 6 Feb 1921
FRENCH TITLE Le Gosse
DIRECTOR AND SCRIPTWRITER Charlie Chaplin
ACTORS Chaplin (tramp), Edna Purviance (mother),
Jackie Coogan (boy), Carl Miller (artist-author), Tom Wilson
(policeman), Henry Bergman (superintendent of the
night shelter), Chuck Riesner (tough), Lita Grey (a flirtatious
angel), Phyllis Allen (woman with the pram),
Nelly Bly Baker (slum nurse), Albert Austin (staying
overnight in the shelter). Contrary to a statement by a French
writer, Sydney Chaplin did not play a representative of
the child-care authority.

An unmarried mother, her baby in her arms, is leaving the
charity hospital. (The father, an artist, has abandoned them.)
Passing a church she sees a young bride coming down the steps
with an elderly bridegroom. A flower from the bride's bouquet
flutters symbolically to the ground. A limousine is waiting outside.
Since it is empty the mother puts her baby inside, with a note:
'Please take good care of my child'. Then hurries away. But the
car is stolen, and when the thieves discover the baby they dump
it in the slums.

Charlie the tramp comes by. Finding the screaming baby, he
is at his wit's end to know what to do with it. A pram standing
outside the nearest shop provides the solution. But just then the
mother comes out. To Charlie's inquiry whether she has lost a
baby she replies that she has not. So Charlie has to take the baby
out again. He tries to put it back where he found it; but a watchman appears, and he has to move on with his burden. He gives
the baby to an elderly man, who in his turn puts it back in the
same pram, whose owner again turns furiously on Charlie.
Resigned, he takes 'the kid' home to his attic hideaway.

Meanwhile the baby's mother has had time for regrets and is
looking for the car. When she hears it has been stolen she collapses.
Charlie finds it troublesome to look after a baby, but provides his
own practical solutions.

Now five years have passed. Charlie and his boy get along well
together. The lad is beginning to be of some use. The boy runs
ahead and smashes windowpanes; Charlie, an itinerant glazier,
brings up the rear and mends them. A policeman sees Jackie
about to fling a stone and guesses something is amiss—a suspicion

122

The Kid, 1921, Chaplin made ckie Coogan a household name. Here e kid as the abandoned baby.

confirmed when Charlie appears with his panes of glass. The couple run away and manage to shake off the policeman. But not for long. On his next glazing job Charlie flirts with the lady of the house, only to discover that she is the policeman's wife. Again Charlie and Jackie are pursued, and only just manage to get home.

In the meantime Jackie's mother has become a famous actress. Missing her baby, she devotes herself to slum charity and in the course of her charity work runs into her own son without realising it. Later she meets the child's father, now a famous fashion designer, at a cocktail party. He tells her he is sorry he ever abandoned her and the child. It is too late, she says. No one knows where the child is.

But at Charlie's place all is peace and happiness. Jackie is running the household and Charlie is taking it easy. For once the vagabond can sit down at a properly laid breakfast table—and teach his 'son' table manners. Jackie sits down in the porch, holding the toy he has been given by the kind rich lady. The tough guy of the quarter comes by and takes it from him. Jackie runs after him and the two boys get into a furious fight in a yard. Charlie, who is passing by, wants to intervene, but is not allowed to. He notices that Jackie, though a good deal smaller, is more than a match for his opponent.

In a pause between rounds the lout's adult brother comes up to Charlie and threatens to beat him up if his little brother gets the worst of it. Whereupon Charlie, for safety's sake, promptly

declares the vanquished the victor. But this does not save him. The big tough knocks holes in the wall and hits a lamp-post so hard that he bends it—without, however, managing to hit Charlie. Jackie's mother appears on the scene. Intervening in her good Samaritan capacity she puts a stop to the fight. And Charlie, for good measure, knocks out the bully with a brick.

Seeing Jackie isn't well, the mother tells Charlie to fetch a doctor. The doctor, a somewhat homespun type, realises Charlie is not the boy's father; that he found him as a waif. The kid, the doctor says, must be properly looked after, and he promises to arrange matters.

Jackie recovers. One day a truck stops outside their home. It has come from the municipal orphanage. The representatives of the child-care authorities, however, do not take Jackie away without a struggle, and have to call the police to help them. When, at long last, the boy is hoisted on to the truck, Charlie, pursued by the police out of his attic, rushes away over the rooftops, takes a short cut, intercepts the truck, flings out the orphanage officials and escapes with Jackie.

Charlie and Jackie do not dare return home. Instead, after Charlie has contrived to get the boy in through a window, they pass the night among thieves in a shelter. Complications multiply. The mother decides to visit the sick boy and is met by the doctor. Among the various papers she recognises her own scribbled note —proof that he is her own long-lost child.

Meanwhile the superintendent of the shelter happens to read in a newspaper that a $1,000 reward has been offered for information about the boy's whereabouts. Recognising Jackie, he picks him up while he is asleep, carries him off to the police station, and pockets the reward. The mother is sent for and Jackie goes home with her.

Charlie wanders about in despair, looking for his boy. Exhausted, he drops off to sleep on his porch, where he dreams of a paradise inhabited by angels—a burlesque ballet scene in which not only Charlie but also the policeman and the 'terror of the streets' have wings and defy the laws of gravity, and where he is reunited with his Jackie. A seductive angel (who turns out to be the thug's wife) tries to vamp Charlie—a notable sequence, inasmuch as the angel is none other than Lita Grey, whom Chaplin married three years later. But there are devils in heaven. The dance turns into a fight, and the feathers fly. Finally, as Charlie is floating away from his pursuers, the policeman shoots him down. He wakes up. It is the same policeman who is standing there, shaking him.

Jackie Coogan as the baby-
up in *The Kid*, 1921.

But only with kindly intent. The boy's mother has realised that Jackie cannot live without his adoptive father. Charlie drives off in a car to her home, where he and the boy are reunited. We are given to understand that the future holds nothing but happiness for them.

The Kid is without question one of Chaplin's most celebrated films and one of the most frequently discussed. Both in 1921 and later it was rapturously received with both laughter and tears. Later critics, not without some justification, have found it a shade too sentimental. But Chaplin was particularly attached to this full-length film. In it Charlie had been able to mirror the dreary circumstances of his own childhood: the attic is said—whether there is any truth in the statement I cannot say—to be a replica of the room in St. George's Road, Lambeth, where Chaplin and his half-brother Sydney had lived with their mother as children.

With *The Kid* Chaplin reconquered his position in the film world, a position which had been a little shaken by the two less successful 1919 films. For Jackie Coogan, who shared its laurels, the film was the springboard to a brief career. His part in *The Kid* was a lucky stroke, no more. Without Chaplin's influence he soon waned.

Today *The Kid* seems rather old-fashioned, and its sub-titles a trifle stiff and pretentious. Even so, it is borne up on genuine feeling. It shows us a Chaplin whose art, without abandoning his own special farce techniques, had matured considerably. Clearly it foreshadows masterpieces to come.

69 The Idle Class (2 reel)

FIRST NIGHT 25 Sept 1921
ALTERNATIVE TITLE Vanity Fair
FRENCH TITLE Charlot et le Masque de Fer
DIRECTOR AND SCRIPTWRITER Charlie Chaplin
ACTORS Chaplin (tramp, temporarily husband of a society
lady), Edna Purviance (his wife), Mack Swain (Edna's
father), Lillian McMurray—mother of Lita Grey—(a
chambermaid), Lita Grey (second chambermaid), Henry
Bergman (sleeping tramp; also a policeman), Allan Garcia
(his neighbour on a bench in the park; also a guest
at the masquerade), John Rand (the golfer; also a guest at
the masquerade), Rex Storey (pickpocket; also guest
at the masquerade).

Charlie and Edna are arriving by train in the fashionable suburb. She is a very superior lady, and as she steps down from her Pullman car, Charlie the tramp crawls out from beneath another. To his usual outfit he has added a bag of golf clubs.

Edna waits in vain for her socialite husband, who is supposed to be meeting her. He has received her telegram, certainly; but has been so exhausted from a party the night before that he has not bothered to do anything about it.

Edna and her two chambermaids drive to the hotel, and Charlie, unnoticed, hitches a lift. On her arrival at the hotel Edna has a painful meeting with her husband, and Charlie drops off the car. Somehow he has lost his trousers. Wandering about the hotel he has to hide in a telephone box as the hotel guests become more numerous.

Edna moves into a room on her own. In a letter to her husband she makes it a condition of their reconciliation that he shall take her to a masquerade ball at the hotel. This part of the film contains an ingenious scene. Her husband is contemplating Edna's portrait and his back, turned to the camera, begins to shake. Is he weeping?—No, just mixing himself a cocktail.

Edna is out riding in the neighbourhood. Charlie is taking a walk by the golfcourse, where he infuriates a golfer by picking up his ball and sending it on its way. It lands in the mouth of a sleeping idler, whence Charlie has quite a job getting it out again. By trampling on his stomach, however, he ejects not only the ball but also several others which have got lost in the same place.

Edna and Charlie meet on a woodland path. At once the vagabond has daydreams of rescuing her, after a wild ride on a mule, from a shying horse. He also dreams of a wedding and a happy family life; we see him holding their first child on his knee. Just as she is disappearing from view he comes to his senses. Charlie's further golfing exploits include a bullseye scored right in the face of Edna's golf-crazy father.

Now we are at the masquerade ball, where Edna's husband appears clad as a knight in armour. Unfortunately his visor gets jammed and when Edna, who is dressed in a superb Madame Pompadour costume and is queen of the ball, looks for him she cannot find him. Soon he appears in a new guise.

Charlie has been sitting on a park bench. A man beside him has had his pocket picked. Unable to see the thief, who is hiding behind the bench, he accuses Charlie. The police are summoned, and Charlie flees—into the hotel and the banqueting hall where the fancy dress ball is going on and where he is at once taken for

Edna's husband, dressed as a tramp. Spending a few quiet moments in her 'husband's' company Edna is pleasantly surprised by his changed manner. But when the real husband sees Charlie flirting with his wife he is furious, and a fight breaks out. Then Charlie insults Edna's father, who is wearing a kilt, for coming to the party without any trousers on. General uproar. Edna faints. Her desperate husband makes renewed attempts to get his helmet off, attacking both Edna's father and Charlie. Charlie, taking pity on him, manages to get his visor open with the aid of a hammer and tin-opener. This of course reveals their true identities, and Charlie is shown the door by the indignant Edna and her father.

Edna, relenting, prevails on her father to run after the outcast. But Charlie, who has had enough of 'high society', plants one of his well-aimed kicks in her father's backside and sets off for fresh fields.

The Idle Class—like *Pay Day* which followed it—was another intermezzo in Chaplin's output, a two-reeler whose qualities lie rather in its mimicry than in its gags. Though it is true that Chaplin has his digs at those levels of society in which he was by now beginning to feel at home, he can hardly be said to settle accounts with them. The idea for the film may have been drawn from *Her Friend the Bandit* a Keystone film (now vanished) in which Chaplin also enters a fancy dress ball and gets thrown out.

70 Pay Day (2 reel)

FIRST NIGHT 2 Apl 1922
FRENCH TITLE Jour de Paye
DIRECTOR AND SCRIPTWRITER Charlie Chaplin
ACTORS Chaplin (worker on a building site), Phyllis Allen
(his wife), Mack Swain (the foreman), Edna Purviance
(his daughter), Sydney Chaplin (Charlie's mate on the job;
also a night-jay and a hot-dog man), Albert Austin,
John Rand and Loyal Underwood (workers on the building
site), Henry Bergman and Allan Garcia (Charlie's
drinking chums)

Charlie is a bricklayer on a building site. When he turns up late for work he tries in vain to appease the foreman with a flower. Charlie tries to make good his negligence by hard work, first in a shaft, where he causes ravages with his spade and pickaxe, and then as a bricklayer. Fast motion produces quite fantastic effects as he juggles with bricks, an activity interrupted by the lunch break. By this time Charlie has already had time to cast longing glances at the boss's beautiful daughter, who has brought her father his lunch basket.

During this lunch break technology celebrates fresh triumphs. A hoist is travelling up and down with extreme precision to the various storeys. Charlie is sitting on a box inside the lift; at the moment when he gets up and steps on to the 'storey', the lift vanishes into the depths; only to come up again beneath him as he sits down. He also conjures, to his own advantage, with his mate's luncheon package and the boss's banana.

But even a long day's work comes to an end; and after a controversy with the boss concerning the contents of his wage packet, Charlie quits the building site. His wages do not remain in his possession for long; outside, his spouse, a grim woman, is waiting for him. Charlie has hidden the banknotes in his hat but she soon finds them. She takes charge of them; Charlie at the same time filches her purse. This gives him the wherewithal for an evening out.

He passes it in the cheerful company of his mates. Late at night, their voices raised in song, they stagger out of the inn into the rain. More water falls on them from above, flung down by the furious occupant of one of the bedrooms.

Before going off home Charlie gives a most effective unconscious performance with his walking stick against some railings. He and his mate (Henry Bergman) both put their arms into the same overcoat, and Charlie under the disapproving glances of a policeman is dragged away in the coat.

The rain falls more and more heavily. Charlie steals his mate's umbrella, but after a solitary walk round the block regrets it, and again swaps it for his own walking stick. There is a long and trying wait for a nocturnal streetcar. When the first tram comes along, a car gets in Charlie's way and prevents him from catching it. Better prepared next time, he clambers ruthlessly over the whole queue to board tram No 2. But the queue forces its way in after him and Charlie is thrust further and further towards the front and out via the front platform. A third time he succeeds no better. The streetcar's passengers are clustered around it like a bunch of grapes, and at the height of Charlie's performance he pulls another passenger's trousers off. Finally he ends up in an itinerant hot dog stall which he mistakes for tram No 4, straphanging from a sausage until the indignant owner throws him off.

At last, in the small hours of the morning, he gets home, only to find his somnolent wife waiting for him with a rolling pin. When he slips into the dining room he finds it is full of cats, one of which makes off with his sausage.

In vain he greases his shoes to prevent them from creaking—just as he is about to turn in, the alarm clock goes off. His wife wakes up. Pretending he is just off to work, Charlie gives her a good-bye kiss, slams the front door and slips back into the bathroom, where at long last he hopes to get some sleep—only to end up in a bath full of washing, from which he is wrathfully expelled by his persecutory wife. He flees.

Pay Day can best be compared with the élite of the Mutual farces. It has the same humorous impact, the same inventiveness, and a superbly caricatured but realistic milieu.

71   The Pilgrim (4 reel)

FIRST NIGHT 25 Feb 1923
FRENCH TITLE Le Pèlerin
DIRECTOR AND SCRIPTWRITER Charlie Chaplin
ACTORS Chaplin (bogus clergyman), Edna Purviance (girl),
Kitty Bradbury (her mother, Charlie's landlady),
Mack Swain (lay worker), Loyal Underwood (dean),
Chuck Riesner (thief), Dinky Dean (rebellious boy),
Sydney Chaplin (his father), May Wells (his mother)
Henry Bergman (Charlie's fellow passenger, the sheriff),
Tom Murray (sheriff number 2), Monta Bell
(policeman), Raymond Lee (real clergyman), Florence
Latimer, Phyllis Allen and Edith Bostwick (female
members of the congregation)

The film begins in much the same way as *The Adventurer*. Charlie has escaped from prison. Hunted by the police, he is looking for a disguise. He finds it in the clothes of a nonconformist minister who has left them on the shore while bathing. Elegant in his new ecclesiastical outfit, Charlie makes his way to the railway station, there to catch a train to some distant spot.

A pair of eloping lovers are looking about for someone to marry them. They catch sight of Charlie. Charlie thinking they suspect him, takes to his heels; but runs into the girl's father, who is pursuing her. Charlie is caught between two fires. To cap all, a suspicious policeman appears.

However Charlie makes good his escape to the railway station where he is determined to take a ticket to 'anywhere on earth'. Just where, he leaves to fate. With averted eyes he sticks a pin into the list of stations. The pin chooses Sing Sing. A second attempt. This time a portly traveller comes between and gets the pin in his backside. Third time lucky. The pin chooses Devil's Gulch. What will be, must be.

Though he has bought himself a ticket, Charlie, out of sheer habit, makes for the undercarriage of one of the cars. There he is discovered by a railway official who suggests he might be more comfortable inside.

Devil's Gulch. Everyone in the little country congregation is anticipating the arrival of a new minister who is to take up his duties. Unfortunately his official dwelling is being repaired, so alternative lodgings have been arranged for him in the house of a friendly religious lady who has a delightful daughter.

The lay worker, Mr Jones, comes to the station at the head of a welcoming committee. At the same moment a telegram arrives from the minister saying he has unfortunately been delayed a week.

Charlie, on the train, knows nothing of all this. All he knows is that he is consumed with desire to get off the train—he has just noticed a 'wanted' photo of himself in the newspaper his fellow-passenger is reading, with a $1,000 reward to anyone who can give any information leading to his capture. At the same moment Charlie notices a sheriff's star on his neighbour's jacket.

The train stops at Devil's Gulch. Charlie gets off. Another sheriff, in full uniform, is waiting on the platform. Charlie, in despair, reaches out his hands for the handcuffs. Instead, he is warmly welcomed both by the sheriff and by his flock, who are just turning up at the station. The new minister has arrived!

Together Charlie and the lay worker go into town. Charlie spots a roll of banknotes in his companion's back pocket. Promptly and unnoticed it changes owners. Now a telegram boy catches up with them. The lay worker's eyesight is none too good, so Charlie reads the telegram for him, inventing congratulations from an unknown lady. The lay worker angrily tears up the telegram. The moment of danger is past.

Now it is time for divine service. After the hymn, Charlie from his pulpit, watching with intense interest as the collection is taken up, takes out a cigarette, but in the nick of time checks himself. Now he has the collection in his possession. He is about to make off with it but is halted by the lay worker. The congregation are still waiting for their sermon. In this critical situation Charlie chooses the story of David and Goliath, brilliantly miming their appearance and the course of their battle, acknowledging the multitude's imaginary applause like a victorious boxer.

The lay worker, however, has recovered the collection. Charlie tries to make good his escape through a vestry window but bumps into the sheriff. Now he puts a good face on it, plucks a rose and is taken along by the lay worker to be introduced to his future hosts. On the way they pass the local bar, Charlie is recognised by one of the customers, the sinister Peter 'Swindler', his former cell-mate. The recognition is mutual. Charlie fears something must be in the wind, and the gaol-bird sees where his mate is lodging

Now Charlie has installed himself in the house, admired his hostess's old family album and made a mental note of her daughter's charms. Over coffee they are visited by a middle-aged married couple with an insufferable little boy who is allowed to

go on the rampage, assaulting his indulgent parents with his fists, knitting needles and glue. After aiming a well-earned kick at this prodigy, Charlie joins Edna in the kitchen, where she is just preparing a plum pudding. The boy slips in and puts his father's bowler over it. Charlie, not noticing the hat, covers it in sauce. Now the time has come to serve up the pudding. Charlie, who is carving it, cannot get his knife through the 'crust'. The father, who has been searching for his hat, furiously takes his leave.

Charlie and Edna are just enjoying a little tête-à-tête by the gate when his former cell-mate makes the opportunity to introduce himself. Invited in, he promptly steals the lay worker's wallet. Charlie conjures it back again; but glimpsing his hostess's mortgage money lying in her chest of drawers, Charlie becomes involved in a duel with his fellow thief for possession of the banknotes. Now the thief has been invited to stay overnight. Both have gone to bed, but Charlie is keeping an eye on the money. In the end the thief outwits him, knocks him out and escapes.

By now the sheriff has found out all about the 'minister's' identity. The ladies, too, are beginning to suspect their lodger of stealing their money.

Meanwhile Charlie has followed the thief to the bar, where he finds the customers being robbed by a group of bandits. Donning a mask, he pretends to be one of the gang, contrives to extract the money from the thief's pocket and flees. After he has given it back to Edna, both she and the sheriff realise the true state of affairs.

Even so—Charlie is a runaway convict and must be put back behind bars. Taking Charlie back to gaol, the sheriff, who is a decent fellow, follows a road along the Mexican border and gives him every chance to make good his escape. He even goes so far as to ask Charlie to fetch him some flowers from the other side. Charlie obeys and docilely returns with the flowers. Not until the sheriff actually pushes him over the border does he take the hint and gratefully sets out on his travels in Mexico—only to find himself caught in a cross-fire between two bandits. He retreats panic-stricken to the frontier. The film ends with him standing with one foot on either side—the eternally precarious situation of the homeless and stateless refugee.

With *The Pilgrim* Chaplin—a good deal later than he had calculated—concluded his engagement with First National. The film was a worthy finale. It poked ferocious fun at American puritanism. Its David and Goliath scene in the church is one of Chaplin's most genial pieces of mime, altogether on a level with his watch scene in *The Pawnshop* and the bread dance in *The Gold Rush*. It has become a classic.

133

impromptu preacher in *The*
1923.

Later Films

As early as the spring of 1919 Chaplin, together with the film stars Douglas Fairbanks and Mary Pickford and the director David W. Griffith, all his close friends, had set up a new company, United Artists, to distribute his own films. Not until October 1922, however, when *The Pilgrim* was finished, were his hands free. Whereupon he immediately set about planning his first film for United Artists. Thanks to the celebrated quartet behind it the company was to become respected, not to say revered, in the international world of cinema; and was to retain its status long after all its four founders had left the arena.

Chaplin signs the document forming United Artists in 1919, as D.W. Griffith, Mary Pickford, and Douglas Fairbanks look on.

72 A Woman of Paris (8 reel)

FIRST NIGHT 1 Oct 1923
ALTERNATIVE TITLE Public Opinion
FRENCH TITLE L'Opinion Publique
DIRECTOR AND SCRIPTWRITER Charlie Chaplin, assisted by
Eddie Sutherland and Monta Bell
ACTORS Edna Purviance (Marie St Clair), Adolphe Menjou
(Pierre Revel), Carl Miller (Edna's fiancé, Jean Millet),
Lydia Knott (his mother), Charles French (his father),
Clarence Geldert (Marie's father), Betty Morissey
(Fifi), Malvina Polo (Paulette), Henry Bergman (hotel
owner), Harry Northrup (footman), Nelly Bly Baker
(masseuse). Chaplin himself puts in only a brief
appearance as a porter.

Marie St Clair is living in a little town, where she has a secret
nocturnal rendezvous with her fiancé Jean, an art student. Her
tyrannical father, who disapproves of their relationship, locks her
out; when Jean's parents, too, turn her away, the two youngsters
decide to try to build up a life of their own in Paris. They meet
at the station, but when Jean goes home to fetch some money he
finds his father has fallen seriously ill and feels he cannot leave
him. At the station Marie misinterprets his telephone message.
Thinking he has abandoned her, she goes on to Paris, alone.

A year later Marie is a well-to-do 'demi-mondaine' supported by
a wealthy and elegant *bon viveur,* Pierre Revel. One evening the
two of them are to meet at the home of an artist friend in the
Quartier Latin. Marie mistakes the apartment and meets up with
Jean and his mother who after the father's death have moved to
Paris.

The couple begin seeing each other again. Jean asks her to sit
for him, and soon he is clear in his own mind that he wants to
marry her even though she is another man's mistress. Marie is
doubtful. Unsatisfied by her loveless existence, however, and once
more attracted to Jean, she decides to quit Pierre, to whom she
is no more than an expensive toy. Unfortunately she overhears a
conversation between Jean and his mother, and imagines that
Jean, under pressure, has again changed his mind. So she decides
to go back to Pierre. Jean takes the blow so deeply to heart that
he commits suicide. In their grief Marie and his mother come
together. They leave the big city to devote their future to looking
after orphans.

Why did Chaplin suddenly make a drama so different from all his films so far? It had long been his ambition to show the world he had more to him than the farce-comedian. Another reason was his wish to give his faithful leading lady, Edna Purviance, a chance to carve out an independent career for herself in films. The idea for the film's heroine, Marie St Clair, the simple small-town girl who conquers the elegant Parisian world—admittedly by entering it by the back stairs—came to him after he had met the beautiful actress and socialite Peggy Hopkins Joyce, who blended sophisticated charm with natural vitality.

Unfortunately, Edna Purviance was unjustly judged in the

role. To the public she was nothing more than Chaplin's slightly insignificant farce partner. Her opposite number, Adolphe Menjou, however, by his perfect rendering of the elegant man of the world, secured his own position in this character part which in the years to come he was to exploit with great success.

The fact remains that *A Woman of Paris,* in spite of its banal plot, has its place in the history of cinema as a remarkable instance of the sophisticated drama. For its day and age Chaplin's sense of nuance and character, simplicity and realism, was most unusual. For other film akers, among them Ernst Lubitsch, his new film dropped a number of hints, which were not lost on them. What its effect would be today is less certain. Times have changed, and so has cinematic technique. But to judge by the expert opinion of those days, and if his 'women' in Paris (1923) and Hong Kong (1967) are weighed in the same scales, Chaplin has learnt little and forgotten a great deal as a film director since he made it.

73 The Gold Rush (9 reel)

FIRST NIGHT 16 Aug 1925
It should be noted that the film had actually already had
a semi-private showing in Grauman's Egyptian Theater in
Hollywood on 26 June, after which it was polished up
by Chaplin, who cut 1,262ft out of the total length of 9,760ft
before releasing it publicly in the Strand Theater, New York.
FRENCH TITLE La Ruée vers l'Or
DIRECTOR AND SCRIPTWRITER Charlie Chaplin
ACTORS Chaplin (independent quester for gold), Mack Swain
(big Jim McKay, also seeking for gold), Tom Murray
(Black Larsen), Georgia Hale (girl), Henry Bergman (Hank
Curtiss), Betty Morissey (Georgia's girl friend),
Malcolm White (Jack Cameron, the local Don Juan)

It is the days of the Klondyke gold rush, in 1898. Among the crowd of men seeking their fortunes in the Chilkoot Pass is Charlie. He is pushing on alone through snow and ice. All unawares, he encounters a polar bear, gets caught in a blizzard, and in the end seeks shelter in a hut occupied by a trapper and violent character by name Black Larsen.

Another fortune hunter is Jim McKay, also out for gold. Overwhelmed by the blizzard, he too finds his way to the hut. There, thanks to his physical strength and eagerly applauded by Charlie, he subjugates Black Larsen.

137

urviance and Adolphe Menjou
man of Paris, 1923.

With Mack Swain, in *The Gold Rush*,
1925.

The hours they pass together during the gale include a number
of ingenious and well-designed gags, such as when the wind blows
the three of them in through one door and out again through the
other; and their struggle over a shotgun, during which Charlie,
no matter how he tries to escape, always finds the muzzle turned
towards himself.

But their food is giving out and Jim has hunger hallucinations.
They decide to draw lots—which of them shall go and seek for
help? The lot falls on Black Larsen. Out in the wilds he runs
into two mounties who are out looking for him. Cold-bloodedly
he shoots them both down.

Inside the hut, meanwhile, Charlie and Big Jim are celebrating
Thanksgiving Day. Charlie tries to cook himself a tasty dinner

from one of his own boots, whose uppers he serves up to Jim while himself sucking sole, laces and nails as if they were the greatest of delicacies.

Jim's hallucinations return with redoubled force. All of a sudden he sees Charlie transformed into a plump bird and chases it with his knife and axe. The panic-stricken Charlie for safety sake gets hold of the shotgun. In the course of a hand-to-hand struggle the gun goes off and kills a bear which has wandered into the hut and with which Charlie is involuntarily grappling. The food question is solved. All is harmony again.

Now the time has come for each of them to go his own way. On the mountainside Big Jim runs into Black Larsen, who has stolen his mining claim. With a blow of his spade the desperado fells Big Jim to the ground, but shortly thereafter meets his own fate in an avalanche.

In the little gold-panning community we meet Georgia, the prettiest girl in town, who is being wooed by the town's he-man Jack Cameron. Charlie turns up, sees Georgia in the saloon, and falls in love with her. But she only has eyes for Jack; and when the latter slights her, she dances with the first man who comes along. This happens to be Charlie, who has just picked up the shreds of her torn-up photo. As he dances with her he hitches his trousers up with a piece of string, not realising the other end is attached to a huge dog. Naturally this complicates their dancing. Jack treats his girl-friend with effrontery. Charlie bravely flies to her defence and with the aid of a heavy grandfather clock puts him out of action.

Needing somewhere to live, Charlie next morning pretends to faint outside a gold-panner's hut. The latter invites him into the warmth for a meal. Afterwards, obliged to sally forth on an expedition, his friendly host asks Charlie to keep an eye on the hut. Georgia and some friends chance to pay Charlie a visit and he falls even more deeply in love. Georgia discovers the shreds of her torn-up photo under Charlie's pillow. The girls think it all very funny. As a practical joke they suggest he invites them out to dinner some time. Charlie is only too willing. They all decide to spend New Year's Eve together.

To finance the dinner Charlie is shovelling snow. He is most methodical, placing the masses of snow he has removed from one doorway in front of the next, thus greatly augmenting his clientèle.

Now all is ready. Charlie has laid the table, with lighted candles, table napkins, place cards and a little parcel for each guest. A roast chicken is cooking in the oven.

But no one comes. Charlie drops off to sleep and dreams that Georgia and he are the life and soul of a wonderful party at which for his guests' delectation he carries out his ever-memorable bread dance on the table, using two French loaves on forks—a most graceful pantomime ballet.

Meanwhile, in the dance saloon, New Year's Eve is being celebrated; and once again Georgia is being wooed by Jack. At the stroke of twelve Georgia fires off a salute—and the shot wakes up Charlie, who at a melancholy distance listens to the singing.

Suddenly Georgia calls to mind the little vagabond's invitation, and proposes to her friends that they all go and visit him. But by the time they get there Charlie has gone down to the dance saloon to watch the party through a windowpane, and Georgia finds the room empty. Seeing the festively decorated dinner table, she is filled with remorse. The joke has gone too far. When Jack, too, goes too far in his attentions, he gets a slap in the face.

Charlie as a succulent chicken in *The Gold Rush*, 1925.

Now the curtain goes up on another drama. Big Jim has recovered from the blow he has received. But he has lost his memory and is wandering about. When he comes to the little town to stake his claim he cannot even remember its whereabouts. In the dance saloon he catches sight of Charlie. His problem is solved. Charlie can lead him back to the hut, and from there he will be able to find his way to his 'mountain of gold.'

ngry enough to eat his shoes in *The*
d Rush, 1925.

Hurt by Georgia's treatment of him but placated by a letter from her, Charlie is at first astonished by Big Jim's eagerness to renew his acquaintance. Then he agrees—as soon as he has had time to declare his love to Georgia he will show him the way back.

Big Jim and Charlie find the hut and install themselves. But during the night a storm blows up. The hut is swept up, sails away, and ends up half hanging out over the brink of a precipice.

Morning. Charlie and Jim wake up and notice that something is wrong. The whole hut is rocking to and fro in the most disquieting manner. There follows an utterly fantastic sequence. Charlie

and Jim, moving to and fro each on his own side of the hut, gradually wake up to their extreme peril. In the end the hut tips over; but a pickaxe roped to it gets stuck in a cleft in the rock and checks its fall.

In the nick of time, as the hut plunges into the abyss, the gold-seekers manage to scramble to safety. The pickaxe, it turns out, has hooked on to Big Jim's golden mountain. Charlie and he are millionaires.

The epilogue: The two elegantly dressed millionaires are the centre of eager attention from the press on board ship on their way home from Alaska. The press photographers ask Charlie to pose in his old tramp outfit. Among the 'tweendecks passengers is Georgia. She has grown tired of Alaska. When she comes across the vagabond, who has tumbled backwards down the ladder while having his photo taken and ended up on a coil of rope, she takes him for a stowaway, and offers to pay his passage. But the ex-tramp, radiant, explains the misunderstanding; and the press photographers get an engagement photo instead.

Even if two other films, namely *City Lights* and *Shoulder Arms*, are close runners up, *The Gold Rush* is 'my' Chaplin film above all others. In it we find everything that is best in Chaplin's repertoire: his pantomime, his biting satire, the human drama, the tenderness. The film is a cavalcade of mankind's hopes and disappointments, a documentary of his deprivations. Goodness, symbolised by Charlie, triumphs in the end. And all the while the sentimental elements are interrupted by logically introduced farce. When the old silent film from 1925 was presented seventeen years later to a new generation (with spoken words and music by Chaplin) it was obvious it had retained its grip on the public. Viewing it today one's verdict is the same. Chaplin has never risen to greater heights than in *The Gold Rush*.

Originally Chaplin's new love, the sixteen-year-old Lita Grey, was to have played the lead; but after some scenes had been shot the role was passed to a more mature actress, Georgia Hale. Instead, greatly to her satisfaction and even more to her mother's, Lita Grey became Mrs Chaplin. A couple of years later the marriage was dramatically dissolved, an event which was to have deleterious effects on Chaplin's next film, *The Circus*.

What gave Chaplin the idea for *The Gold Rush*? It was born, it seems, while he was spending a weekend with his friend Douglas Fairbanks. The two film stars were sitting looking at stereoscope slides, some of which were taken from Alaska and Klondyke. One, taken in the Chilkoot Pass, showed the lemming-like trail of

tle tramp on the snow covered
ins of Alaska, in *The Gold*
925.

fortune-hunters climbing the heights under difficult conditions. This was the picture which sparked off Chaplin's film. As for the documentary elements, he took them from a book about a group of pioneers who had got lost on their way to California, and had been snowed in high up in the mountains of Nevada. Many died of cold and hunger and some had even turned to cannibalism. It was this real-life tragedy which gave Chaplin the idea for the film's hunger scenes and his leathery Thanksgiving dinner. The setting once established, the comic and dramatic details presented no great difficulties. And soon the epic he had so long dreamt of was being made.

74   The Circus (7 reel)

FIRST NIGHT 7 Jan 1928
FRENCH TITLE Le Cirque
DIRECTOR AND SCRIPTWRITER Charlie Chaplin
ACTORS Chaplin (tramp), Allan Garcia (circus director),
Merna Kennedy (his stepdaughter, a circus rider),
Harry Crocker (Rex, the trapeze artist), Betty Morrisey
(lady who vanishes), George Davis (conjurer), Henry
Bergman (old clown), Steve Murphy (pickpocket),
Stanley Sanford (ringmaster), John Rand (his assistant)

The film begins with a circus scene in which we witness a poor piece of clowning and see the bareback rider Merna after an unsuccessful turn. Her stepfather, the director of the circus, is displeased. He strikes her and bawls at the clowns. The public has begun to desert them.

Charlie the tramp arrives in the circus area, a curious observer. In the crowd a pickpocket has just snatched an elderly gentleman's wallet. To escape suspicion, which has fallen on him, he stuffs it into Charlie's pocket and shadows him to get it back again.

Cunning and heartless, the hungry vagabond robs a little child of a sausage he is eating, seated on his daddy's arm. But then, discovering the wallet, has a solid meal. The rightful owner catches sight of his property, summons a policeman, and Charlie flees, as does the thief.

Chased by the police, both rush into the hall of mirrors, where they quarrel comically. To dupe the police, they pretend to be automata outside the Funny House. However, Charlie is discovered and again has to take to his heels—this time into the circus ring,

arlie on a precarious perch in *The*
rcus, 1928.

where he makes a great if involuntary hit with the public in a
magical transformation act.

He is taken on—officially as an odd job man—by the circus
director, gets to know the girl, and finds that an act in which he
flees from a restive donkey has made him into the circus's great
public attraction. After some unpleasant moments shut up in the
lion's cage he escapes thanks to the girl, with whom he is now in
love. Charlie's happiness is at its height when a rival appears. He
is Rex, a newly engaged trapeze artist, a magnificent specimen of
a man. It is with him the girl, Merna, is in love.

At a safe distance from Mother Earth, Charlie has been secretly
trying to learn the difficult art of tightrope walker. One evening
Rex suddenly disappears and Charlie is given a chance to show his

girl. The director orders Charlie to perform his perilous act high up under the big top. Charlie secretly takes all necessary measures for his own safety—a scene-shifter undertakes to manoeuvre the rope attached to a safety belt round Charlie's waist—and brilliantly commences his act. But catastrophe is at hand. A bunch of monkeys have broken loose. They attack the tightrope walker, who suddenly realises his safety belt has come undone.

By the skin of his teeth Charlie manages to reach the platform and on his cycle rushes straight down into a nearby shop. When he comes back. Charlie gets some rough treatment from the circus director and is promptly fired.

Merna, weary of her stepfather's brutality, wants to leave her

circus life in the company of the vagabond. But Charlie, who sees she still loves Rex, seeks him out, talks him into marrying the girl and even makes him a present of the engagement ring he has bought for her. He is best man at the wedding. To keep his stepdaughter and Rex, the circus director is obliged to mend his ways.

The circus moves on. Charlie is graciously invited to accompany it but knows he is superfluous and declines. For a while he is left sitting by himself in the sawdust hole with the crumpled paper star. Then, plucking up his courage, he twirls his walking stick and sets out optimistically for the unknown—the classic Chaplin finale.

The Circus is a remarkable film in many ways. Some critics have done it less than justice, for the most remarkable thing of all was that it was ever completed. In that nightmare year, 1926, when shooting began, innumerable difficulties had arisen for Chaplin. After *The Gold Rush* Chaplin was at the height of his fame. More than ever before he had to try to rival himself. But just then his stormy second marriage to Lita Grey, was on the rocks. For an artist who above all needed peace and quiet to collect his thoughts, the situation was becoming chaotic, not to say catastrophic. Already his unsuccessful marriage (it ended with a divorce in 1927) had begun to be ventilated in painful detail in the press; and public opinion — not least of the feminine variety — was becoming indignant.

To cap all, some sand got into the equipment when more than two-thirds of the film had already been shot, and the shootings had to be broken off. Chaplin fled to New York and had a nervous breakdown. Not until the divorce had gone through, after almost a whole year of inactivity, could he collect himself and complete the film—in itself perhaps one of his most remarkable achievements.

But there were other troubles, too. His old ensemble had been scattered—of all the foreground figures from his Mutual period, 1916-17, only Henry Bergman, who plays the old clown, was left. Under prevailing conditions *The Circus* also became an unusually expensive film, a good deal more so than *The Gold Rush,* for which the estimates had been $700,000. *The Circus* cost $900,000. Chaplin had had a complete circus constructed for the purpose, including a small zoo; and all of this had to be kept in being for a whole year and more. Finally, his wife Lita Grey had strong opinions about his choice of leading lady. She talked Chaplin into engaging her friend Lerna Kennedy. Lerna was not a particularly gifted actress, and her contribution is at best acceptable.

147

lion tamer, in *The Circus,* 1928.

A hungry Charlie eyes a tempting
sausage, in *The Circus*, 1928.

It is true there is less poetry in *The Circus* than in a number of Chaplin's earlier and later films. But in many respects *The Circus* is a crossroads in Chaplin's production. Its subject is the martyrdom of art—in this case the clown's martyrdom—which it presents in a manner which could hardly be more naked. It is Charlie Chaplin the tramp who enters the action, but Calvero, from *Limelight,* who leaves it.

When the little fellow is chased into the arena by the police his terror and agony are transformed into an act to amuse the public. Another terrifying experience—his flight from the donkey—is the source of another public success. In *Limelight,* Calvero takes a melancholy view of the artist's circumstances and of the world that has been his. He shows up his merciless public for what it is. *The Circus* comes to the point more directly. Even if its technique is derived from the earlier and shorter Chaplin farces, it stresses the element of sheer terror—a terror intimately connected with the demanding nature of an audience.

I know of no Chaplin film from which the entertainment industry has afterwards borrowed more freely. The scene in the fairground's hall of mirrors was modified long afterwards for thriller effect by Orson Welles in his *Lady from Shanghai.* The William Tell number and the shaving scene in the circus ring have enriched many later circus comedies. Indeed Chaplin himself was exploiting a genre which flourished in the twenties and whose prototype was the German director Du Pont's *Variété.* Chaplin transformed it into scenes of comic terror. For the fact remains: even if the little clown's Pagliaccio tears are mainly tears of bitterness, *The Circus* is still a *funny* film.

It successfully made its comeback in 1969 after Chaplin had re-edited it. In this version Merna Kennedy swings from the trapeze under the big top to music newly composed and an introductory song sung by Chaplin himself.

75 City Lights (9 reel)

FIRST NIGHT 6 Feb 1931
FRENCH TITLE Les Lumières de la Ville
DIRECTOR AND SCRIPTWRITER Charlie Chaplin
ACTORS Chaplin (the tramp), Virginia Cherrill (blind girl),
Florence Lee (her granny), Harry Myers (eccentric
millionaire), Allan Garcia (his butler), Hank Mann
professional boxer), Henry Bergman (mayor; also a janitor),
Albert Austin (street-sweeper; also shady character),

149

The terrified little tramp, in *City Lights*, 1931.

Stanhope Wheatcroft (head waiter in the night club),
John Rand (old tramp), James Donnelly (foreman at the
refuse removal station), Eddie Baker (referee in the ring),
Robert Parrish (newsboy), Jean Harlow (extra)

A peace monument is being unveiled. As the dust sheet is removed,
Charlie who is taking a nap against it is also revealed. After a
certain amount of trouble he manages to make himself scarce. At a
street corner he meets up with a blind flower girl, who takes him
for a millionaire. It transpires that she lives at home with her
granny.

Later, at night, Charlie comes down to the harbour, where he
finds a tipsy gentleman who wants to take his own life by tying one
end of a rope to a large stone and putting the noose round his

150

n *City Lights*, 1931, with Henry
Myers as the eccentric millionaire.

neck. Charlie intervenes, to his own undoing. Both end up in the
water, but scramble ashore. Charlie accompanies his new-found
friend, (who turns out to be a millionaire) to the latter's luxury
flat, where he is treated to strong liquor. Again he prevents the
millionaire (depressed because of a divorce) from committing
suicide, this time with a revolver. But finds an enemy in his butler.

Now the millionaire brightens up, suggests that they go out to
a night club together. In the night club Charlie's behaviour causes
chaos. He slips up on the polished floor, sets fire to a lady's dress,
confuses the spaghetti on his plate with the streamers which come
floating down from the ceiling, intervenes in an apache dance and
dances wildly.

Morning. The two of them are zig-zagging home in the
millionaire's Rolls-Royce. At first the butler throws Charlie out;

151

Thieves are about to end Charlie's bliss, in *City Lights*, 1931.

but at his friend's orders he is fetched back again. Charlie is lent some money and the car. Again he meets the blind girl, buys up her whole stock of flowers and drives her home. But by the time he returns, the millionaire has sobered up and can remember nothing at all of what has passed. Charlie is pushed out by the butler and goes away disappointed.

Next time they meet the millionaire is again drunk. He welcomes his 'friend' with open arms and arranges a party in his honour. At the party Charlie again puts his foot in it, mistakes a bald head for an ice cream and swallows a whistle. Morning brings an unpleasant awakening. Finding Charlie beside him in his double bed, the millionaire does not recognise him at all. Once again he is chucked out.

Charlie, disillusioned, makes for the street corner to meet the

Reduced to throwing a "fixed" fight,
n *City Lights*, 1931.

blind girl, but cannot find her. So he looks her up in her home
where he hears she is ill and in need of proper attention. Charlie
undertakes to pay for it, and takes a job as a street-sweeper. This
brings him into fresh troubles, with among other things a pro-
cession of circus animals.

Charlie goes on playing the millionaire as far as his purse
permits. He buys the girl food, and upon reading in a newspaper
that a famous eye specialist from Vienna is in town, decides to pay
for the operation. A great deal of money is needed. The girl and
her grandmother have not paid their rent and are being threatened
with eviction. Charlie returns to his street-sweeping but is fired for
turning up late.

Instead he allows himself to be enticed by an offer of 'easy
money' in a fixed boxing match. All he has to do is to be a stand-in.

His opponent is a thief who at the last moment has to run from the police. He is replaced by a massive fellow of enormous strength, who is perfectly agreeable to taking on Charlie on the terms already arranged: winner takes all. After an extremely funny match, Charlie is knocked out.

Straying through the city, he again runs into the millionaire. Just back from a trip to Europe, he is, as usual, tight. Their reunion is of the heartiest, and once again Charlie is invited up to

City Lights, 1931.

his flat, where the millionaire gives him money to help the girl. But just as he has stuffed the banknotes into his pocket thieves break in, knock the millionaire down and when Charlie summons the police, flee. The police arrive and naturally suspect Charlie of being the thief, the more so as the millionaire, when he comes to, is as sober as a judge and refuses to acknowledge his friend. Charlie manages to get away, rushes to the girl and gives her the money. In the end, picked up by the police, he serves a lengthy prison sentence.

He comes out again and is wandering about in town. On one occasion he is the target of a malign joke by some newspaper boys, outside a flower shop. The shop is owned by the girl, who has undergone the operation and regained her sight. At first she laughs at the ridiculous little tramp; but then, pitying him, comes out and gives him a rose. It dawns on her that the shabbily dressed little vagabond is none other than her benefactor. But Charlie is realistic—they are still living in different worlds, though this time the roles are reversed.

City Lights is proof that Chaplin was right in regarding mime as crucial to his art. At a moment when Hollywood was enthralled by the new talkies, Chaplin insisted that his new film should have no spoken words. But he did give it a music track, for safety sake composing the music himself. The shooting was by no means without friction. Chaplin temporarily fired his faithful assistant director Harry Crocker, and after a row took away the millionaire's role from Henry Clive and gave it to Harry Myers—an action which cost him thousands of feet of wasted film. He was even on the verge of changing his leading lady, as he had done in *The Gold Rush,* but Virginia Cherrill, a beautiful blonde, was taken back into favour.

After two years' work the film was ready. Its triumph was obvious. Once again Charlie, in a 'silent', had quelled the uproar of the talkies all round him. *City Lights* offered what was perhaps his most original story-line, constructed round the blind flower girl with pathos and romance, tenderness and feeling. The film is not excessively sentimental, and his audiences smiled through their tears.

City Lights is one of Chaplin's greatest films—none of his later productions were to reach the same heights. Revived in USA in 1950, its new first night was the scene of almost sensational enthusiasm. A new generation, sold on the talkies, had to admit that Chaplin, king of the silents, could still assert himself. Since then this film has run successfully in USA and Europe as part of a massive world revival of the best Chaplin films.

76　Modern Times (9 reel)

FIRST NIGHT 5 Feb 1936
FRENCH TITLE Les Temps Modernes
DIRECTOR AND SCRIPTWRITER Charlie Chaplin
ACTORS Chaplin (tramp), Paulette Goddard (working class
girl), Henry Bergman (café owner), Chester Conklin
(mechanic), Allan Garcia (manager of a steel works),
Lloyd Ingraham (governor of the prison), Louis Netheaux
(drug addict), John Rand (gaolbird), Stanley Sanford (man
working next to Charlie on the moving belt),
Hank Mann (his cell mate), Mira McKinney (wife of
the prison chaplain)

The film opens with a shot of a flock of sheep jostling in their sheep pen. The parallel follows instantly: an army of industrial workers on their way to work. In the upper storey sits the manager (played by Allan Garcia, the brutal circus director in *The Circus*). On a TV screen he can keep an eye on all parts of the factory. Tempo is the watchword of the day.

Charlie is a worker on the moving belt. His job is to tighten up bolts. All the time he is being urged on by the foreman to keep up with the belt. Even when he goes to the washroom he has the manager's eye on him. The management wants to try out a new method of shortening the lunch hour. A lunch machine serves the 'client' what he wants. Charlie is selected as guinea pig, but while serving corn on the cob the machine goes wrong and his meal becomes a nightmare.

At work again after lunch Charlie simply cannot keep up. Dragged into the machinery among gigantic cog wheels, he automatically goes on tightening up bolts. Free, again he starts his own private revolution, turns wheels and throws levers as the fancy takes him. Apparently out of his wits, he performs a graceful ballet with some perilous acrobatics—and is taken away for psychiatric treatment.

Charlie's stay in hospital does wonders. He is discharged with orders to eat well, get all the sleep he needs and above all not become excited. Unfortunately he needs a job, and just now the labour market is depressed, factories are closed. On the street Charlie picks up a red flag which has fallen off a lorry carrying explosives. When he waves it to draw attention to the fact, he suddenly finds himself at the head of a 'red' demonstration that has just come round a corner. The police arrest him as its ring leader.

To support her family a young girl, a cheeky little creature from the slums, steals a bunch of bananas from a case on board a freighter. We see her in her home sharing out her booty with her unemployed father and motherless younger sisters.

In prison, Charlie finds himself in bad company. A drug addict has managed to smuggle in some 'snow' under his prison clothes and when the drug squad makes a razzia during the lunch hour he hides the powder in a salt cellar. Unsuspecting, Charlie takes a

th Paulette Goddard, in *Modern*
nes, 1936.

Again man against machine in *Modern Times*, 1936.

pinch of salt and is astounded at its effect on him. So too is his fellow prisoner who has earlier tyrannised Charlie but on whom Charlie now gets his own back. After lunch Charlie gets lost in the corridor, and when he tries to enter his cell finds it locked. Two prisoners have revolted and locked up their warders. Charlie takes them, too, by surprise. Strengthened by the powder, he knocks out the escaping convicts and releases the warders. His reward is a cell with all modern conveniences. Summoned to present himself before the prison governor, he is told he has been released.

Meanwhile, in the girl's home, tragic events have occured. Her father has been killed in a riot, and the child care authorities have come to take charge of her sisters. The girl herself has managed to make herself scarce.

classic scene with Chester Conklin,
Modern Times, 1936.

With a letter of recommendation from the prison governor
Charlie applies for a job in a shipyard and is accepted. The foreman orders him to find a large wedge, and so he does—beneath the
hull of a ship which is still being built! Taking a sledge-hammer
he knocks it loose: whereupon the half-built ship slides down the
slips into the harbour and sinks. And Charlie gets the sack.

Obviously civil life is altogether too fraught with risks. Charlie
longs for his comfortable cell and does what he can to get back
into it. He meets the girl, whom he knocks down as she is trying
to run off after grabbing a loaf from a baker's van. The police
intervene. Hoping he will be gaoled, Charlie declares it was he who
stole the bread. But witnesses say it was the girl, and she is arrested.

Charlie tries again. This time he goes into a snackbar, orders a large portion without being able to pay for it, and grabs some cigars in passing. This time he finds himself in the lock-up, with the girl. She seizes a chance to escape. Charlie, who has changed his mind about the drawbacks of freedom, follows her. Both get away. In the outskirts of the city they are dreaming of a happy family life in the country, when they are frightened away by a policeman.

The night watchman in a large department store has broken his leg. Charlie hears about it, applies for the job, and gets it. He admits the girl. They stock up with goods from the food counters and then amuse themselves in the toy department. In a game of blindman's buff Charlie does some perilous roller-skating—not realising that the well railing has been taken away for repairs. While Charlie, still on roller-skates, is going his rounds the girl indulges in all the pleasures of a luxurious bedroom in the furniture department. He disturbs a gang of burglars, but recognises his former cell mate as their leader. Whereupon they all pass a happy night together at the store's expense.

Next morning Charlie wakes up on a counter in the drapery department where he has been found by the personnel. He is taken away by the police. Ten days later he is let out. The girl is standing there waiting for him. She has found them a home, admittedly only a ruined shack by the river bank, but still a home.

Charlie is determined to get back to work. Seeing a newspaper report that the factory has reopened, he rushes there and is allowed to start work again. A magnificently funny sequence follows in which he tries to set the huge machine in motion. The foreman gets caught among the cogs, passes down the whole transport system, and 'comes out' at various points before Charlie finally succeeds in mastering the situation. Alas, his job is short-lived. A new strike is declared. Once again he is out of work.

Meanwhile the girl has got herself a job as a dancer in a little cabaret and when after a few weeks, she and Charlie meet again she is in clover. Beautifully dressed, she is already drawing big audiences. She gets him taken on on trial as a waiter by assuring the management that he can sing. Waiting on the customers, he runs into various troubles; on one occasion Charlie and his loaded tray are caught up and swept away by the crowd of dancers. After getting stuck in the chandelier, the roast duck becomes the inebriated guests' rugby ball.

But real trouble comes as a result of his promise to sing. The girl and he work up a little song together and Charlie, to help himself remember the words, writes them down on one of his loose

160

he fadeout. Charlie and Paulette
oddard in the final scene of *Modern
imes*, 1936.

cuffs. But at the critical moment he makes such a dramatic gesture
that the cuff flies off his arm. Obliged to improvise new words, he
does it in a fantastic language of his own (a satire on the linguistic
confusion of the age). No matter. Charlie is a great success. Alas, in
the very moment of triumph the girl is nabbed by two men who
have long been searching for her on behalf of the child care
authorities. She contrives to slip out of their clutches. Charlie
covers her retreat. And once again the couple flee.

Next morning they are sitting at a cross-roads on a country road.
Shaking off their depression, they set off hand in hand—a variant
of Chaplin's earlier classic exits.

When the talkie film was first introduced Chaplin had declared:
'Talkies? I detest them. They come to ruin the world's most
ancient art, the art of pantomime. They annihilate the great
beauty of silence'. No one can say he did not fight a gallant rear-
guard action. Though it has a musical soundtrack and Chaplin
himself sings the cabaret song 'Titina' (the Cuff Song) *Modern*

161

Times, too, is a 'silent'—the last full-length silent film ever made.

In it Chaplin attacks the violence done to human freedom by the Machine Age. His satire on industrialism, at the beginning, is both drastic and exquisitely funny. But the tempo of *Modern Times* is too uneven for it to reach the standard of *The Gold Rush* or *City Lights.* As entertainment, of course, it has great qualities; also a charm and a spontaneous warmth of feeling whose origins lie in the new relationship between Chaplin and Paulette Goddard. But in the pattern of its farce and in its settings *Modern Times* is too deeply rooted in an earlier Chaplin epoch to be called original. It will chiefly be remembered for its brilliant singing scene, one of Chaplin's very finest pieces of mime. To discern communist sympathies lurking behind the film's social satire seems far-fetched, though many detractors have both sought and found evidence for such an accusation.

77 The Great Dictator (12 reel)

FIRST NIGHT 15 Oct 1940
FRENCH TITLE The Dictator
DIRECTOR AND SCRIPTWRITER Charlie Chaplin
ACTORS Chaplin (a Jewish barber, also Tomania's dictator
Adenoid Hynkel), Paulette Goddard (Hannah the
Jewish girl), Jack Oakie (Benzino Napaloni, Dictator of
Bacteria), Reginald Gardiner (Schultz), Billy Gilbert
(Herring), Henry Daniell (Garbitsch), Grace Hayle
(Madame Napaloni), Carter de Haven (Bacteria's ambassa-
dor), Lucien Prival (an officer), Eddie Gribbon and
Hank Mann (storm troopers). In the ghetto: Maurice
Muscovitch (Mr Jaeckel), Emma Dunn (Mrs Jaeckel),
Bernhard Gorcey (Mr Mann), Paul Weigel (Mr Agar), Chester
Conklin (the man being shaved), Leo White (a barber)

'This is a story of a period between two World Wars—an interim in which Insanity cut loose, Liberty took a nose dive and Humanity was kicked around somewhat.'

With these words Chaplin opens *The Great Dictator.* The scene is a battlefield in France in World War I; the time, 1918. Though it is losing the war the state of Tomania, whose double cross is its appropriate national symbol, is still aiming to reach Paris. One of the soldiers is a little Jewish barber, an artilleryman. His attempts to fire a gigantic Big Bertha-type cannon are fruitless. Its first shot

e little barber meets the storm
oopers in *The Great Dictator*, 1940.

hits a lavatory. The second shell drips out of the end of the barrel.
The barber is ordered to defuse it, but the shell spins round and
round. Whichever way he turns, it points at him (reminiscent of
the struggle with the shotgun in *The Gold Rush*). In the ensuing
offensive the barber manages to drop a hand grenade inside his
uniform, strays over to the enemy lines in the fog, and yet survives.
One of Tomania's pilots makes a forced landing and is injured.
The barber saves him, and the two make a perilous flight before
finally being shot down. They land, unhurt, in a dung heap.

Peace breaks out. The barber, suffering from total amnesia, is in
hospital. The years pass—years graphically illustrated by newspaper headlines: Dempsey's victory over Willard, Lindberg's
flight across the Atlantic, the Great Depression, and finally 'Hynkel

seizes power in Tomania'. Now the barber has come out of hospital. While Hynkel in a hoarse, inarticulate falsetto which perfectly mimics Hitler's, is inveighing against democracy, freedom and the Jews, the barber goes back to his abandoned shop. The masses meanwhile are jubilant. Even the microphones bow their 'Heil Hynkel'. When the dictator exhorts his people to tighten their belts, the belt of the obese minister of war, Herring (Goering) snaps. Exit Hynkel, adorned with flowers given him by little girls. As his car drives down the avenue even the statues make a 'Heil' salute.

In the city ghetto, however, the atmosphere is depressed, the economy wretched, and fear of Hynkel's storm troopers great. As usual the girl Hannah, who has lost her parents in the war, is going her rounds with the laundry. But already the street has become the storm troopers' playground. In the next scene the barber is being sought by the authorities—the officer whose life he saved twenty years earlier wants to get in touch with him. Meanwhile his rescuer has found his barber's shop full of cats and the dust and spiders' webs of two decades. This puzzles him. But he soon cleans it up and resumes his profession.

Even when some storm troopers paint the word JEW on his shop window he still fails to grasp anything of what is going on and wipes the word out, which involves him in a fight. But at her window Hannah comes to his aid, and the aggressors are knocked out.

New storm troopers appear. They surround the barber and make ready to hang him from a lamp-post. At that moment the officer Schultz—now one of Hynkel's closest associates—chances to pass by. He recognises his former passenger, and saves him.

In Hynkel's palace, meanwhile, the dictator and his henchmen are planning to invade the neighbouring state of Austerlich. But an invasion costs money. To finance it they will have to borrow from the great Jewish financier Epstein. The Jewish terror will have to be temporarily shelved. In the palace Hynkel caricatures Hitler by climbing up a curtain (variation of biting a carpet). Intoxicated by his power he plays ball with a globe—he is going to conquer the entire earth—a fantastic ballet scene, whose end is that the globe bursts like a balloon and the dictator collapses in a fit of hysterical weeping.

Meanwhile the barber, his double, has become a close friend of Hannah, who allows him to do her hair. He also shaves an elderly client (Chester Conklin, veteran of so many Chaplin farces), to the accompaniment of one of Brahms's Hungarian dances.

164

But the idyll is brief. Epstein refuses the loan. Hynkel flies into a rage and orders the terror against the Jews to be stepped up. Now the concentration camps are waiting. When Schultz advises against such barbarism he is arrested but manages to escape into the ghetto, where the barber and Hannah are hiding from their persecutors.

The Jew-hunt is depicted in almost documentary fashion, to an accompaniment of Hynkel's gurgling proclamation coming over the city's loudspeakers. Confusion spreads in the ghetto and turns to panic, all very far indeed from Chaplin's earlier comic modes of self-expression. Hiding in an attic the barber and Hannah see his barber shop go up in smoke. Schultz prevails on the barber to join in a secret conspiracy to blow up Hynkel's palace. Lots are drawn to choose the man who is to do the job. Each has to eat a cake, in one of which is a coin. Hannah, however, who dislikes the whole plan, has put a coin into each of the cakes, and there is a hilarious scene in which each member of the group tries to conceal his own coin.

But now the newspapers are saying that Schultz and the barber are wanted men. The Gestapo is after them. Dressing up as golf-playing tourists they try to escape over the rooftops, but are caught

As Hynckel in *The Great Dictator*, 1940.

Adenoid Hynckel, the rabble rouser, in
The Great Dictator, 1940.

and taken away to a concentration camp. Hannah succeeds in
crossing the frontier into Austerlich, where she settles in an
idyllic spot in the countryside.

Hynkel is just about to launch his invasion of Austerlich when
he hears that his rival Napaloni is about to do the same. Napaloni,
conceited, boastful and loquacious, is invited to a conference in
Tomania. He arrives with his wife and attendants, and the two
dictators' meeting turns into a ludicrous competition. Each tries
to outdo the other and make him feel inferior. The struggle for
power reaches its climax at a banquet where Hynkel has to dance
with that mountain of flesh, Napaloni's wife. The buffet supper
which follows is chaotic. After this trial of strength the two
dictators agree on a plan of invasion.

denoid Hynckel, the pensive
eamer, in *The Great Dictator*, 1940.

To mask their intentions and calm the neighbouring nation,
Hynkel goes duck-shooting near the frontier. At the same time the
barber and Schultz steal some uniforms and escape from the nearby
concentration camp. When Hynkel, in his Tyrolean get-up,
capsizes his rowing boat and has to swim ashore, the men who have
been sent to find him take him for the barber, seize and silence
him. On the road, meanwhile, the barber has run into advancing
storm troopers who acclaim him as their dictator. He is forced to
accept the part. As Hynkel, he drives into Austerlich in a motor-
cade. All along the road posters announce that the ghetto has been
stormed and all Jewish property confiscated. The invaders even
reach Hannah's hideaway, where they maltreat the refugees.

In the capital of Austerlich the masses have assembled to listen to the dictator's speech. After the foreign minister Garbitsch has condemned the notions of liberty, equality and democracy, it is the dictator's turn. Into his long speech—quite different from any the masses have been expecting—the little barber puts his all.

This rhetorical finale lasts for six minutes—Chaplin has been criticised for it, as a breach of style and even, in the circumstances, a banality. But in this concluding vignette Chaplin felt he had to give direct expression to his loathing for dictatorship and violence and preach his sermon on the blessings of peace. As such, it deserves to be quoted. We have taken the liberty of borrowing the whole speech from the film's sound track.

I'm sorry, but I don't want to be an Emperor—that's not my business. I don't want to rule or to conquer anyone. I should like to help everyone, if possible—Jew and Gentile, Black men, White.

We should all want to help one another; human beings are like that. We want to live by each other's happiness, not by each other's misery. We don't want to hate and despise one another. In this world there is room for everyone, and the good earth is rich, and can provide for everyone. The way of life could be free and beautiful.

But we have lost the way. Greed has poisoned men's souls; has barricaded the world with hate. It has goose-stepped us into misery and bloodshed. We have developed speed, but have shut ourselves in. Machinery that gives abundance has left us in want. Our knowledge has made us cynical. Our cleverness, hard and unkind. We think too much, and feel too little. More than machinery we need humanity. More than cleverness we need kindness and gentleness. Without these qualities life would be violent, and all would be lost.

The aeroplane and the radio have brought us closer together. The very nature of these inventions cries out for the goodness in man, cries out for universal brotherhood, for the unity of us all. Even now, my voice is reaching millions throughout the world—millions of despairing men, women and little children, victims of the system that makes men torture and imprison innocent people.

To those that can hear me I say, do not despair. The misery now that is upon us is but the passing of greed, the bitterness of men who fear the way of human progress.

Hate of man will pass, and dictators die, and the power they took from the people will return to the people. And so long as men die, liberty will never perish.

Soldiers, don't give yourselves to brutes, men who despise you and enslave you, regiment your lives, tell you what to do, what to think and what to feel, who drill you, diet you, treat you like cattle, use you as cannon fodder. Don't give yourselves to these unnatural men—machine men with machine minds and machine hearts. You are not machines. You are not cattle. You are men. You have the love of humanity in your hearts, you don't hate. Only the unloved hate—the unloved and the unnatural.

Soldiers, don't fight for slavery, fight for liberty. In the 17th chapter of St Luke it is written: 'The Kingdom of God is within man'—not one man, nor a group of men, but in all men. You the people have the power, the power to create machines, the power to create happiness. You, the people have the power to make this life free and beautiful, to make this life a wonderful adventure.

Then in the name of democracy, let us use that power. Let us all unite. Let us fight for a new world, a decent world that will give men a chance to work, that will give youth a future and old age a security.

By the promise of these things brutes have risen to power. But they lied. They do not fulfil that promise—they never will. Dictators free themselves, but they enslave the people.

Now, let us fight to fulfil that promise. Let us fight to free the world, to do away with national barriers, to do way with greed, with hate and intolerance. Let us fight for a world of reason—a world where science and progress will lead to all men's happiness. Soldiers, in the name of democracy, let us unite.

The Great Dictator, Chaplin's first talkie, was not finished until the autumn of 1940. By then the horrors of war and concentration camps were already grim realities. In many people's eyes this made the whole subject too delicate, and the farcical and satirical elements seemed dubious. Even so, *The Great Dictator* played an important role as a mouthpiece for the hopes of the free world. Like Walt Disney's propaganda films it made the dictators, Hitler in particular, look ridiculous.

78 Monsieur Verdoux (12 reel)

FIRST NIGHT 11 Apl 1947
FRENCH TITLE Monsieur Verdoux
DIRECTOR AND SCRIPTWRITER Charlie Chaplin
ACTORS Chaplin (Henri Verdoux, a bank employee with
many aliases: Varney, Bonheur, Floray), Mady Correll
(Mona, his wife), Allison Roddan (their son), Martha Raye
(Annabella Bonheur), Ada-May (Annabella's chambermaid),
Isobel Elsom (Marie Grosnay), Marjorie Bennett (her
chambermaid), Margaret Hoffman (Lydia Floray)
Helen Heigh (Yvonne), Irving Bacon (Pierre Couvais),
Almira Sessions (Lena Couvais), Edwin Mills (Jean Couvais),
Virginia Brissac (Charlotta Couvais), Eula Morgan
(Phoebe Couvais), Marilyn Nash (the girl), Robert Lewis

(Maurice Bottello Verdoux's neighbour), Audrey Betz
(Madame Bottello), Charles Evans (Morris, the detective),
Fritz Leiber (clergyman), Barbara Slater (florist),
William Frawley (inspector of police), Bernard J. Nedell
(superintendent of police), Edna Purviance (an extra)

Chaplin dons the guise of an insignificant Parisian bank clerk to
illustrate the world of the depression and the war. M Verdoux
is a man who takes the trade cycle into his own hands, having
convinced himself that what the world can do unpunished on a
vast scale, the individual may do so on a small one. In either case
it is mostly a matter of business.

Monsieur Verdoux, 1947. Chaplin as
the fashionable art dealer.

Monsieur Verdoux is a mass-murderer who has left a rather unremunerative job in the bank to support himself and his family on such monies as he can get out of gullible middle-aged ladies whom he bigamously marries without either his wife or his son having an inkling of what he is up to. All have fallen for his charm and have handed over their assets—and thereby lost their right to exist.

Verdoux has a double nature. On the one hand he is the tender husband and father who is so taken up with his business affairs that he only sporadically has time to spend down in the country in the bosom of his family. On the other, he is the coldly cynical exploiter of women's affections; the perfect criminal, who at his own place

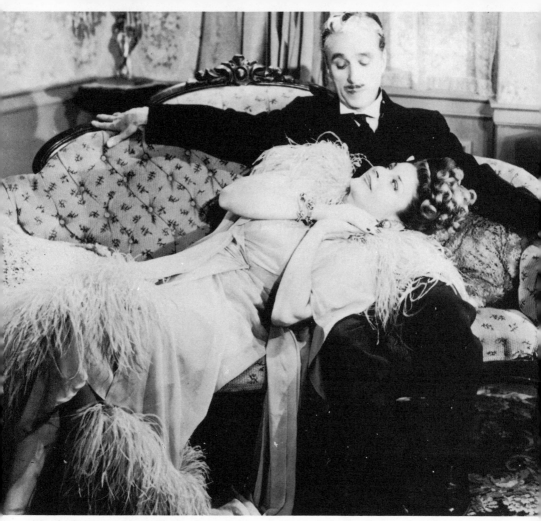

Martha Raye, as Annabella Bonheur, is captivated by the lover in *Monsieur Verdoux*, 1947.

in the outskirts of Paris has installed an incinerator to get rid of his victims and who invests their money on the Stock Exchange.

The Paris police are receiving one report after another of women disappearing. So far twelve have vanished. An elderly lady, Lena Couvais, is trying to trace her sister Thelma who has gone away to marry a certain M Varnay, but of whom nothing has been heard for the past three months. Her bank account has recently been drained.

Monsieur Varnay, alias Verdoux, is seen in his garden busying himself with his roses; he is a gentleman who would not hurt a worm and there assiduously avoids stepping on one. To his house comes a wealthy widow, Marie Grosnay. She is thinking of buying the property. Instantly she becomes a highly desirable 'prospect'. Alas, she is reluctant, and must therefore be put on ice.

Verdoux returns from Paris. Some bankers give him disturbing

Monsieur Verdoux, 1947. The man of
affairs.

news about the state of the stock market. Hastily he draws out all
his reserves. One of his 'wives', Lydia Floray, a lady who has seen
her best days, lives in a country town under the erroneous belief
that her husband is away in Indo China. He relieves her of this
illusion, and by talking about an imminent bank crash panics her
into immediately withdrawing all her money. Whereupon Lydia,
too, is liquidated.

After a harmonious visit to his legitimate family, Verdoux
resumes his business affairs. Now he visits another of his 'wives':
Annabella Bonheur, a jolly and energetic society woman of
maturer vintage. She has been causing him trouble by insisting on
managing her own affairs. This can no longer be tolerated. From
a neighbour, an owner of a drugstore, Verdoux has heard of a
poison which leaves no trace. He obtains some. At that moment he
hears that Annabella has taken all her money out of the bank, and

173

is just in time to prevent her from investing it in a new firm. He decides to act quickly.

But first he must try out the new poison. In Paris he finds a suitable guinea pig in the shape of a young girl whom he meets one evening and whom he invites up to his flat. But her story is so sad that Verdoux is deeply touched. She has been in prison, and has also had to take care of her husband, a war invalid who has just died. Verdoux abandons his 'test'. Instead he gives the girl some money. Shortly thereafter he is visited by an inquisitive detective out for an arrest, and tries the poison out on him instead. It works, and on the train back to Paris his victim dies. His prisoner Verdoux takes his keys, unlocks his handcuffs and gets off the train at a country station.

All set to serve her a lethal potion, Verdoux returns to Annabella. Unfortunately his bottle gets mixed up with another containing hair tint bought by the housemaid. Annabella sips the evil-tasting hair tint; and the housemaid rubs the poison into her scalp and goes bald. Annabella is fond of her own life. When Verdoux tries to drown her from a boat he falls in himself and is rescued by his 'beloved'.

Now Verdoux concentrates on the conquest of his earlier acquaintance, Marie Grosnay, whom he has long been bombarding with flowers and other tokens of his sentiments. In the end she yields and agrees to marry him. But Annabella happens to be invited to the wedding reception. Verdoux, horrified, leaves in a hurry.

Newspaper placards announcing the failure of banks, European crisis, meetings between Hitler and Mussolini, bombs over Spain, etc, carry us forward a few years—years which have left their mark on Verdoux. His legal and much loved wife has died, and so has his son. Business is bad. Crossing the street one day he is within an inch of being run over by a magnificent car.

Its owner recognises him as the elegant gentleman who once invited her up to his flat, gave her money and thereafter had lent her a helping hand. In the interim she has formed a relationship with a plutocrat, an explosives manufacturer. Wishing to repay her debt, she drives her benefactor to the Café Royal. He just has time to tell her of his difficulties when he is recognised by that shadow from his past, Lena Couvais, who is visiting the café in the company of her nephew. Monsieur Verdoux realises the game is up. After getting his former protégée out of the way he hands himself over voluntarily to the police.

Among the spectators at his trial he has only one friend: the girl. Grieved to see what is going on, she cannot believe he is the devil in human guise he is represented as being. As for Monsieur Verdoux himself, he lays the whole blame on a profit-greedy society whose outcome can only be war. Compared with the legalised and honourable mass-murder going on all over the world, his own little series of murders, punishable though they now are, have been mere nothings.

A reporter interviews him in prison. Surely he will concede that crime does not pay? Verdoux's reply is embittered and philosophical: 'Not on a small scale'. He is executed. But his executioner is the whole world. Such is Monsieur Verdoux's—and Chaplin's—point of view.

As a Chaplin film *Monsieur Verdoux,* certainly, is different. All traces of the tramp have vanished, what remains is the satirist with a novel and ferocious cynicism.

It is not only society and its mechanisms which Chaplin attacks, but also the evil inherent in mankind itself—notably in those of its parasitic members who make money out of crime, the crime of flinging our world into a new conflagration, and who thus provide the forcing ground for such existences as Verdoux's—or of the French mass-murderer Landru, on whose career the film is based.

Without a doubt *Monsieur Verdoux* is Chaplin's angriest attack on society. It has naturally therefore also been the one his detractors have been most at pains to parry. It was not a box office success and it received mixed reviews. *Verdoux,* however, is not only Chaplin's most controversial film; it is also one of the most interesting. As a study of our epoch it will hold its place in time to come. Those who regretted the loss of his tramp figure—as many did—must consider the context. The passing of the years had made him an impossibility.

79   Limelight (13 reel)

FIRST NIGHT 23 Nov 1952
FRENCH TITLE Les Feux de la Rampe
DIRECTOR AND SCRIPTWRITER Charlie Chaplin
ACTORS Chaplin (Calvero, the old music hall artist),
Claire Bloom (Terry, the girl), Sydney Chaplin Jr
(Neville, a youthful composer), Nigel Bruce (Postant, the
ballet impresario), Buster Keaton (old comedian),
André Eglevsky (Harlequin), Melissa Hayden (Columbine),
Charles Chaplin Jr and Wheeler Dryden (clowns),
Marjorie Bennett, Snub Pollard, Loyal Underwood and
Geraldine, Michael and Josephine Chaplin (extras)

175

It has been said that Edna Purviance is one of the audience in the film's ballet sequence, but Chaplin has denied it. In his memoirs he says that the last time he met his former leading lady was in 1947, while shooting *Monsieur Verdoux*. By 1952 she was probably suffering from the cancer which killed her in 1958.

Calvero, the old comedian, has been a celebrity of the music halls at the turn of the century. Today he is living on as a venerable has-been in a single London lodging room, embittered by memories of his former glory. But one day he comes home and smells gas. Tracing it to a neighbouring flat where a young girl is living, he forgets his own troubles, breaks in, finds her unconscious, and looks after her until she comes to. The girl, Terry, tells him how, after vainly trying to make her way as a ballerina, she has tried to commit suicide. Calvero gives her fresh courage to try again, and himself dreams of once again performing his star turns.

Calvero the clown, in *Limelight*, 1952.

Buster Keaton, in *Limelight*,

Fortune smiles on Terry. She is 'discovered', and is given a leading role in a new ballet by the young composer Neville whom she recognises. He had been a customer of a music shop where she used to work, and from which she was given the sack, having tried to make good out of her own pocket the loss she had incurred by giving him too much change.

Terry cannot return Neville's love; she imagines she is in love with Calvero whom, in spite of the age gap between them, she wishes to marry. But Calvero sees it is impossible. After the old comedian has failed to make a comeback in a minor music hall, Terry talks her own impresario into giving him a chance in the ballet; but after a short while Calvero has to be laid off. He is simply not up to it. Subsequently, the impresario realises who he is and tries to find him. In vain, Calvero has vanished.

One day during the war Neville catches sight of Calvero among a group of street buskers. He tells Terry and she talks him into letting him have another try. The impresario is putting on a

The broken hearted clown, with Claire Bloom in *Limelight*, 1952.

charity show. It is here that the old star is given his chance. Calvero is a success. He makes his comeback in a double bill with one of his colleagues from former days (played by Buster Keaton). The audience calls for more, and Calvero follows up his success. But tragedy follows. Over-excited by his own happiness the old clown has a heart attack. From the wings he just manages to follow his adored Terry dancing the star role in Neville's ballet. Before it is over, Calvero is dead.

With *Limelight* Chaplin's career as an artist comes full circle. It was from London's variety world he had first emerged as a youthful mimic to create a unique position for himself in films. In the guise of an ageing but still brilliant comedian living on his memories he returns to the same world—the world of London in 1914.

In its own way *Limelight* can be regarded as Chaplin's film about himself, if not in its outward action at least in the thoughts, feelings and places it presents. In it he finds expression, in his own inimitable way, for his love of his art and of the world of the stage which the old variety artist Calvero says he so hates but which is nonetheless indispensable to him.

No one was better capable of subtly acclaiming yesterday's actor, faithful to the last, while at the same time telling us a nostalgic but charming story about the autumn and epilogue of an actor's days. There is much of the old Chaplin: his tenderness, his genuineness of feeling, his social pathos. Calvero is of the same flesh and blood as the solitary little man who had once danced the can-can with a loaf of bread in *The Gold Rush*. But above all there is a discernible link with *City Lights*. Here as there, we are entertained to a melodious ballet-like theme, in which Chaplin the composer expresses something of himself—a simple typically Chaplinesque melody.

Limelight is eloquent of the comradeship of the footlights, and the art of living for one's art. It is Chaplin's settlement of account with life. *Limelight* should have been the end of his film career; the rest seems meaningless and irrelevant.

Farewell to America

In his memoirs Charlie Chaplin has given his own account of the circumstances which forced him and his family to leave the United States in September 1952. Here it is enough to say that it was Chaplin's pronounced individualism, his loathing of all compromise when he knew he was in the right, his (to the American public) undeniably provoking series of marriages and his incapacity to cope satisfactorily with the press, which were the source of all his difficulties.

The citadels of power which Chaplin had challenged in some of his films and also in his vulnerable private life, always watched by a sensation-hungry yellow press all over the world, were exceedingly dangerous ones. He had aroused the moral indignation of the bigoted but powerful American women's clubs. His satire *The Pilgrim* had turned certain religious circles against him: *Modern Times* had challenged the world of industrialists. And when, finally, he dared to hold the whole of society responsible for the deeds of the mass-murderer Monsieur Verdoux, and then declared his dealings with close friends, whatever their political opinions, to be no one's business but his own, then there was nothing for it but for him to take the consequences. He was accused of being a belligerent communist. The American Legion went on the warpath against his *Monsieur Verdoux,* and he found himself in trouble with the immigration and tax authorities.

This persecution by the moralists was the last straw. Chaplin shook the dust of an ungrateful America from his feet—that America which had once taken him to its heart but which could never forget, among other slights, that he had never become an American citizen.

It is from this bitterness (even though relationships were afterwards 'normalised' and Hollywood took him back into its embrace in 1972) that he produced *A King in New York* (1957), his first film as a European resident. Produced by himself, it was released through Universal.

80   A King in New York (11 reel)

FIRST NIGHT 12 Sept 1957
FRENCH TITLE Un Roi à New York
DIRECTOR AND SCRIPTWRITER Charlie Chaplin
ACTORS Chaplin (King Shahdov of Estrovia), Maxine Audley (his
wife), Dawn Addams (girl), Michael Chaplin (boy), Oliver
Johnston, Jerry Desmond, Phil Brown, Harry Green, John
McLaren, Alan Gifford, Shani Wallis, Joy Nicols, Johan Ingram,
Sidney James, George Woodbridge, Robert Arden, Lauri
Lupino-Lane, George Truzzi

King Shahdov of Estrovia has fled his own country to the USA
after a revolution. He is quick to realise that in America his
royal title is an asset to be exploited. His Majesty is in dire need
of cash. Through a young woman employee of a TV company he
accepts an offer to advertise certain products, to some of which
he is allergic—eg, whisky, which sticks in his throat during a TV
show.

Once again Chaplin has come as an immigrant to 'the Land of
the Free'. This time it is to be the pawn of the celebrity racket
and to be confronted with the wildest excesses of the American
show business. He takes under his wing a young boy who has left
his school when his parents have been summoned to appear before
the Committee for Unamerican Activities. When a fire breaks out
Chaplin has the personal pleasure of aiming the fire-hose at that
committee's members. But he has had enough of USA, and goes
home to his own country.

A King in New York does not altogether lack Chaplinesque
qualities. There is his superb mime in a brilliant scene about the
difficulties of making conversation; also in the sequence where,
having had his face lifted, he watches a cabaret show, but does not
dare to laugh—until the whole work of the face-lifter's art disinte-
grates. His satire on TV, films and the rock-and-roll craze is funny,
full of wicked details, for example, the TV apparatus which is
hidden behind a phoney library and the ingenious hit refrain on
the theme 'When I think of a million dollars I get tears in my eyes'.

But when Chaplin has his son Michael stand up, tense and
precocious, and hysterically lecture us with his father's social
criticisms, then Chaplin not only misses his target but turns the
film into thoroughly inartistic polemics. Chaplin's bitterness has
got the better of him. After the film's light-hearted introduction
one has an unpleasant feeling that *A King in New York* was made

A King in New York, 1957, Chaplin's
last starring film.

in a state of affect. Progressively disintegrating it reaches new lows
in Chaplinesque comedy, for example, the peeping-through-the-
keyhole scene. Despite its aspirations to social satire, the film as a
whole cannot be relished by any admirer of Chaplin.

81   A Countess from Hong Kong (12 reel)

FIRST NIGHT 2 Jan 1967
FRENCH TITLE La Comtesse de Hong Kong
PRODUCER Jerome Epstein
DIRECTOR AND SCRIPTWRITER Charlie Chaplin
ACTORS Marlon Brando (Ogden Mears, a wealthy diplomat),
Sophia Loren (Countess Natascha), Sydney Chaplin Jr
(Harvey, Mr Mears' best friend), Tippi Hendren (Martha),
Patrick Cargill (Hudson), Margaret Rutherford (Miss
Gaulswallow), Michael Medwin (John Felix),
Oliver Johnston (Clarc), John Paul (captain), Angela

Scoular (society girl), Angela Pringle (baroness), Jenny Bridges (countess). Charlie Chaplin is glimpsed in a minor extra role as an elderly steward.

The American multi-millionaire and diplomat Ogden Mears is taking the boat home to USA via Hong Kong, Kobe and Honolulu. When the ship puts into Hong Kong he passes an agreeable evening in the company of a young woman who claims to be a Russian countess. Waking up next morning in his luxury suite, he finds her hiding in a closet. At first furious, he agrees to help her remain hidden on board. After a protracted game of hide-and-seek with various complications all over the ship, the time comes for a happy ending.

Chaplin seems to have got the idea for his Russian countess's adventures in 1931 in the course of a trip to the Far East. In Shanghai and elsewhere he met poverty-stricken Russian emigrés. During World War II their descendants had moved to Hong Kong, though they were certainly no better off there.

From this bright idea he succeeds in making little more than a French-style bedroom comedy with sentimental episodes between the whirligigs. Far and away the film's best scene is an intermezzo in the cabin of that movie veteran Margaret Rutherford. She is the very image of a ruin in luxury wrappings. But no matter how luxury-wrapped this Chaplin film is as a whole, there can be no question but that as a film it is poverty-stricken. Its directing is conventional, wholly lacking in the spontaneity and imagination that were formerly Chaplin's hallmark. But why should we demand miracles from old age, even from the old age of a genius?

The Freak

In the autumn of 1969 Charlie Chaplin began planning yet another full-length film, his eighty-second. Bearing the working title *The Freak*, it was to have been about a girl born with wings. Chaplin created the leading part for his daughter Victoria, then eighteen, and also to launch Josephine, her younger sister by two years. Jerome Epstein was called in as co-producer. Though the story is written by Chaplin, it contains no role for himself. According to a statement of Epstein's in the spring of 1970, however, the film has been shelved 'because of technical problems'. At this time of writing it seems dubious whether it will ever actually be made.

Chaplin's 'Unknown' Films

Among Chaplin's films from the year 1915 was a two-reeler, *The Champion*, containing a remarkable little guest performance by 'Broncho' Billy Anderson (1882–1971), the first cowboy hero of the silver screen. He plays an enthusiastic ringside fan. Broncho Billy put his money on the right horse. In 1915 he held a managerial position in the Essanay company, which had just secured Chaplin's services. Chaplin paid for Billy Anderson's contribution to *The Champion* by himself appearing in a saloon sequence in *His Regeneration,* one of Broncho Billy's one-reeler Westerns. Chaplin is wearing his usual tramp outfit and the scene is a farce interpolated in the middle of a dramatic story about a thief's conversion. Totally unmotivated as an episode and brief though it is, it is funny and typical of Chaplin. As soon as he leaves the dance floor the main drama continues.

This was by no means Chaplin's only 'guest performance' outside his own series of films. A number of film stars, among them Mary Pickford, Douglas Fairbanks and Charlie Chaplin, placed themselves at the disposition of the 1918 American War Bonds campaign. Chaplin's contribution was a little one-reeler. As far as I know it has only recently been noticed in Europe, on TV. It consists of four sketches. Chaplin appears in all of them. Edna Purviance is the object of Charlie's passion, which ends up at the altar. Oddly enough, this is the only Chaplin film, apart from a dream sequence in *The Idle Class,* in which he and Edna actually get married.

One of Chaplin's most faithful colleagues, Albert Austin, plays a friend who wants to borrow money, and Chaplin's half-brother Sydney—as in *Shoulder Arms*—plays the Kaiser. *The Bond* makes subtle use of the stylised black-and-white background. After illustrating the bonds of friendship, of love (a scene in which Chaplin hangs up his walking stick on the crescent moon and has

184

an arrow shot through him by Amor) and of marriage, we are brought to the most important bond of all, the Liberty Bond. The Kaiser tries to rape the Goddess (Statue) of Liberty. But American soldiers from all branches of the Service, equipped with Chaplin's money bags, come to her rescue. The final twist is when Chaplin, armed with a Liberty club, knocks out the Kaiser and shows the audience the way to victory. Some 660ft of effective propaganda!

That autumn (1918) Chaplin appeared in a similar film (half-reeler) for the British War Loan, together with Harry Lauder. Also extant from this campaign is a documentary scene in which Mary, 'Doug' and Charlie are seen speaking at a war loan meeting. Afterwards Charlie is seen shadow-boxing with the former world champion, Jack Dempsey, and conducting a military band. The latter episode, strangely enough, is virtually a copy of the introductory scene in *A Night Out* (1915), which was regrettably cut at an early stage. These documentary pictures can be seen in the Chaplin cavalcade *The Funniest Man in the World* (1969).

Chaplin has yielded to inducements to appear in brief scenes in other stars' films. Thus he pops up in Douglas Fairbanks' *The Nut* (1921), is in the crowd in James Cruze's *Hollywood* (1923), and also appears in a short scene in the Marion Davies film *Show People* (1928).

Spurious 'Chaplin' Films

Down the years the distributors of Chaplin films have not been particularly scrupulous. From 1915 onwards, numbers of so-called Chaplin films appeared and it is not always easy to sort out the genuine. The name 'Charlie' and 'Charles' was always appearing in advertisements, often with a drawing of the Chaplin figure; but when the audience turned up, they could find that the leading role was played by some imitator: a Billy Ritchie, a Billy Reeves or a Billy West. In the years 1915–20 Billy West emulated the Charlie figure in a whole series of 'Chaplin films'. In many cases the distributors were at least decent enough to add the words *'Imitation à la Charlie Chaplin'* to the titles. Even a film advertised as an imitation was a draw, such was Chaplin's popularity.

One example of this exploitation of the Chaplin motif is the film *The False Chaplin* (1921). Its contents are described as follows in the archives of the Swedish board of censors : 'Elsie West breaks off her engagement because of her admiration for Charlie Chaplin. She writes to him begging to meet him. Her letters to her fiancé and to Chaplin get mixed up. The fiancé dresses up as Chaplin, introduces himself into her family, behaves in an incredibly crude and uneducated manner at table, and gets thrown out. When the fiancé appears in his own guise he and the girl are easily reconciled.'

An innocent enough tale, one might think; but the Swedish censor did not think so in 1921. It banned the film totally with its usual motivation 'brutalising'. It is the only bogus Chaplin film ever to be banned in Sweden.

Not only imitators were making hay in the sunshine of Charlie Chaplin's popularity. The activities of caricaturists too were stimulated by its steady increase from 1915 on. During the war years the *New York Herald Tribune,* for instance, syndicated a daily strip cartoon of Chaplin adventures, which until 1917 was drawn by Elzie Segar—followed by, among others, Ed Carey and (probably) Gus Mager.

More or less simultaneously the film industry awoke to Chaplin's cartoon possibilities. A long series of Chaplin cartoons was released, many of them based on the Charlie-Mabel-Fatty trio. The most prolific cartoonists were I. C. Terry and Pat Sullivan.

For many years one particular Chaplin film has been a source of irritation to all who have searched for it: *In The Park*. Anyone ordering an eight-millimetre copy no matter where from, has always received the wrong film, namely *Caught in the Rain*. The simple fact is that the latter film was rechristened for the reduction print market, with the result that today two films are circulating under the name *In the Park*: the real one made in 1915, and the wrongly entitled one, made in 1914. Unfortunately it is almost always the wrong one that is in circulation.

In the export market Chaplin's films have appeared under a host of strange titles. This was notably so during the 1920s. Again and again Chaplin films would be released under two or three different names, and the public who had gone to see a new Chaplin masterpiece found they had already seen it. Many Chaplin films were also shown in wretchedly cut copies. A prime example of this was the classic *Shoulder Arms*. As late as 1970 (in a German copy in two parts) it was being shown in Europe with a total footage of only 1,772ft. The original ran for 3,143ft.

But if Chaplin has been treated in a slovenly manner in Europe, even greater violence has been done to him in America. In his exhaustive Chaplin biography (1952), Theodore Huff, the most eminent of Chaplin's chroniclers, describes the goings on. In USA it was not just a question of incongruous or more or less authentic films, but of intentional forgeries. Small scenes would be taken out of old Chaplin films—mostly the Keystone productions, the 1914 films never having been copyrighted—and put into a new context with the aid of freshly shot material, Chaplin's role being played by an imitator. This gross malpractice was particularly rife in the years 1917–18, when Chaplin had reached the height of his popularity.

Among queer titles may be mentioned *The Fall of the Rummy-Nuffs, The Dishonour System, One Law for Both, Charlie in a Harem* and *Charlie Chaplin in A Son of the Gods*. In the last of these, authentic Chaplin scenes were mingled with clippings from the film *A Daughter of the Gods* (1916) made by the world-famous swimmer and variety artiste, Anette Kellerman. Audiences were treated to the spectacle of Charlie leaping about among mermaids.

All these malpractices were rooted in the Chaplin hysteria of the years 1915-19. It drew in its wake not only imitators, strip cartoons and cartoon films, but also Chaplin souvenirs in the shape of figurines, statues, masks, cut out albums, etc. It was a small foretaste of the gigantic industry which was afterwards to grow out of Walt Disney's dream factory.

Over the years, then, many people have played fast and loose with Chaplin's films, and all too often they have got away with it. But sometimes Chaplin has taken his exploiters to court. Two of the gravest assaults on his artistic integrity were *Triple Trouble* and *Carmen*. The tangle over the first of these is the more complicated. Its starting point is a full-length film that was never completed.

In 1915, Chaplin—at an astronomical fee—had just installed himself with the Essanay company. He had the idea for a full-length film called *Life*. It was to be an ambitious satire, with a serious social message. Though he got quite far with it, it was never allowed to be completed—the Essanay management had realised the tremendous draw of Chaplin's two-reelers and did not want him to waste his time and talent on a film which might not be such good box office. Chaplin had to submit, and went on making shorts. Much footage had already been shot, however, and some use had to be found for it. Certain scenes were used in *A Night in the Show* (at the beginning), and a whole sequence (the scenes in the night shelter) was intended for *Police,* but also had to contribute to *Triple Trouble*—a piece of patchwork which also utilised unused scenes from other Essanay films, notably *Work,* whose entire final scene it impudently steals. New footage was shot, doubles being used where necessary, and the puzzle was pieced together with the aid of Leo White, who besides acting in Chaplin films also had talents as a director. Theodore Huff strikingly illustrates the forgery: in 1915 Edna Purviance (in *Life*) throws a wet rag through a door; in 1918 it hits Leo White (newly shot scene); and in 1915 (*Life*) he throws it back at the cook.

In February 1916, Chaplin, unsuspecting of what was afoot, left Essanay, and by 1918 Essanay had carried out its plan. A miraculously clever piece of editing produced the forgery. Viewers found it well-nigh impossible to see the joins. Essanay advertised it as 'A new Chaplin film'.

The *Carmen* forgery I have already described in my chapter on the Essanay period. It was almost as nasty a piece of counterfeiting as *Triple Trouble*.

Chaplin Cavalcades

Chaplin's films have been linked up in cavalcade programmes of varied length, with differing success. Sometimes the distributor has cut them together any old how, a short scene here, a longer sequence there. But examples also exist of cavalcades that magnificently exemplify Chaplin's artistic development.

The roughest exploiter of Chaplin film footage was the Essanay company, for which he worked, from 1915 into 1916. After he had left them for Mutual in 1916 they put together something they called *The Essanay-Chaplin Revue,* an anthology of the films *The Tramp, His New Job* and *A Night Out.* This might not have mattered had not the company advertised the group as having a single story line, in which in the course of his wanderings the tramp saves the girl (Edna Purviance), loses her and returns to town, where he seeks work in a film studio and finally ends up in the dubious company of Ben Turpin, his drinking companion.

Unquestionably the three films were ingeniously selected and when run *en suite* hang together tolerably well. Even so, the scheme was not quite honest. It should not be confused with the first cavalcade film to be shown in Sweden (in February 1918), which is also called *The Charlie Chaplin Revue.* This was divided into three parts consisting of 880ft, 915ft, and 1,145ft and containing the greater part of *The Jitney Elopement, The Champion* and *His New Job.* Another cavalcade of no less than seven reels (one of the longest so far) was released in Britain in 1918 under the title *Chase me Charlie,* with Essanay scenes edited together by Langford Reed.

Another British product is *Comedy Cocktail,* a two-reeler pivoting on *A Night in the Show,* but also containing excerpts from *Laughing Gas, His Musical Career* and *The Champion.* This film had a music track—something that is wrong with Chaplin's old silents; the violent underlining of gags by sound effects infallibly destroys both the atmosphere and the comedy. The subtleties of Chaplin's mime are lost. The method has nevertheless been utilised in a number of pot-pourris of much later date. *Chase Me Charlie* contains excerpts from *Making a Living, His New Job, The Tramp, A Woman, Work, The Bank* and *Shanghaied;* whilst *Comedy Cocktail* takes a more panoramic view of the years 1914–17 and contains fragments of no fewer than 20 one and two-reelers. It also interpolates documentary pictures of great interest, finely commentated by Douglas Fairbanks Jr.

Naturally, *The Chaplin Revue* of 1959, having been released by Chaplin himself with his own freshly composed and sober music, makes a high-class Chaplin film (1,115ft). It comprises fairly complete versions of *A Dog's Life, Shoulder Arms* and *The Pilgrim.*

But Chaplin cavalcades are legion. In Sweden, alone no fewer than twenty-four have been presented, including the farce pot-pourris *When Comedy was King* and *Days of Thrills and Laughter,* in which Chaplin had to share with a number of other comedians. Among the best may be cited *Chaplin Festival* (1943), which contained longer sections from *The Immigrant, The Adventurer, The Cure, The Count* and *Easy Street, Merry Go Round* (1962) (*By the Sea, Triple Trouble, The Tramp* and *The Champion*), and *Thirty Years of Fun* (1963) (*Easy Street, The Pawnshop, The Floorwalker, The Face on the Bar Room Floor* and *The Rink*).

Chaplin's Collaborators

Chaplin has rarely anything to say about his collaborators' contribution to his films. This egocentric attitude that 'my films are my work and mine alone' needs to be qualified.

Creative genius though he was, Chaplin would not have got far without the help of original and clever collaborators and fellow actors. In his later and more demanding productions, with their purely dramatic elements, he has been more dependent on technically trained assistants. Chaplin himself, no matter how great his successes, can hardly be reckoned among the great film directors. Behind the camera his qualities reveal themselves only in his instruction of actors and his ability to inspire them intuitively. The prime instance here was Jackie Coogan in *The Kid*. Chaplin owes a debt of gratitude to many people, above all to two women who were crucial to his film career: Mabel Normand and Edna Purviance. As women, they were diametrically opposed types.

Mabel Normand (1894–1930) was born in Boston and began her career in New York as a photo model. A talent scout employed by the Vitagraph Film Company spotted the beautiful and exuberant Mabel, who had talents in swimming, riding and archery. For a year she appeared in their films, after which she came to D. W. Griffith and Biograph, where she met Mack Sennett. They played together in several films, and when Sennett, who had become wholly fascinated by Mabel's charms, established himself in Hollywood in 1912, Mabel went with him. She was a veritable elixir, a source of inspiration for the prolific farce-maker. It was she who hit on the idea of his famous police corps; she also flung the first pie, and thus contributed that sticky substance to the film farce. When, in 1913, Chaplin came to Sennett, Mabel was already established as his brilliant comedienne, an exuberantly vital star, with an inexhaustible vein of comedy. That she afterwards came to be called 'a female Chaplin' was no coincidence. They had much in common, including the gift of mimicry.

Mabel Normand alone grasped Chaplin's peculiar genius and possibilities from the outset. During the first period in the Keystone studios Chaplin was a reserved and taciturn member of the crazy wild gang. Mostly he kept to himself, and was by no means sure he had chosen the right outlet for his art. Mabel adopted Chaplin, encouraged him, and acted as his liaison with the boss Mack Sennett whom she could twist round her little finger. It was Mabel Normand who succeeded in convincing him that Chaplin was a card to bet on.

After Chaplin's debut in *Making a Living* Sennett was dissatisfied, and is even said to have half repented having recruited him from the Karno variety show. Mabel whom Chaplin has called 'a remarkable woman' was brought into the directing, and there were some heated tugs of war; but gradually Chaplin was given freer hands, and his collaboration with Mabel as his leading lady was to prove decidedly fruitful.

Altogether they played in eleven films before Chaplin left for Essanay in 1915 and Mabel, with the help of her faithful admirer Mack Sennett, went on to make an independent career for herself in full-length features—a career tragically and prematurely broken off. She was involved in one of the most publicised scandals of the twenties, in connection with the murder of the film director William Desmond Taylor, in 1922. That she was never actually accused of this murder was neither here nor there. Unfortunate circumstances linked her name with it. Her films were boycotted. Her career was at an end. She died of tuberculosis at the age of thirty-six.

A similar scandal in connection with a murder put an equally tragic and unjustified end to Fatty Arbuckle's career. In both cases a public idol was brought down by adverse publicity—the sort of publicity from which Chaplin too was to suffer.

Edna Purviance (1894–1958) was born in Paradise Valley, Nevada. When Chaplin noticed her in 1915 she was working as a shorthand typist in San Francisco. She was a blonde Juno. Although she had no experience either of stage or screen, party because her statuesque figure made Chaplin's physique seem even more spindly and pathetic, and partly because she seemed to embody that chaste romanticism which, in an evil world, was the object of the little vagabond's dreams, she was the perfect leading lady for him. She adapted herself wholly to his requirements.

Chaplin never had a written contract with Edna. But in film after film, year after year, she stayed with him. From *A Night Out* (1915) onwards she played the leading female role in thirty-five of his films. Unfortunately the last of these (if we ignore the one in which she played an extra) was not only the most expensive, but also boomeranged on her. She functioned admirably in short farces, where she was her master's willing instrument. But the dramatic primadonna role which Chaplin, by way of reward, created for her in *A Woman of Paris* (1923) was, for Edna personally, a failure; and for his later long films Chaplin had to find other leading ladies. In 1946, however, when he was making *Monsieur Verdoux*, he tried to induce Edna to make her comeback in an important part as Madame Grosnay. Reluctantly Edna came to the studios and made some test shots. But it was clear to both herself and to Chaplin that she was not up to the part. Chaplin supported Edna, who was already on his list of pensioners, right up to her death from protracted cancer in 1958. But though he was deeply attached to her and they were close friends, his feelings for her, despite all that has been suggested to the contrary, were never of the romantic sort.

Three more names deserve to be cited 'for long and faithful service', from Chaplin's list of actresses. First, *Minta Durfee,* Mack Sennett's pretty soubrette, who played with grace and temperament in so many amorous but tough Keystone farces. She plays in at least eleven Chaplin films as well as perhaps having other as yet undiscovered minor roles to her credit. She was married to Fatty (Roscoe) Arbuckle, who had also been engaged by Mack Sennett. Her husband died at the age of forty-five in 1932, but Minta Durfee was still alive in 1970.

Alice Davenport (b 1853) and *Phyllis Allen* were women of riper years and played within a certain format. As a termagant wife Phyllis Allen repeatedly gave many fiancés in the audience occasion to go home and look before they leaped.

The actor among all his collaborators who stood closest to Charlie, of course, was his half-brother *Sydney Chaplin* (1885– 1965). Chaplin's respect for and attachment to Sydney, four years his senior, arose not merely from blood ties or gratitude for all the help and support he had received from him in childhood. Sydney was also to be an immense help to him for the future, as among other things, a financial adviser, as well as an actor. When first engaged for *A Dog's Life,* 'Syd' had already created a solid name for himself in film comedies. He deserves specially honourable mention for his double role in *Shoulder Arms*, where he plays the American sergeant as well as the Kaiser, and even more so for his leading role in *A Submarine Pirate*, a four-reeler made for Mack Sennett in 1915 after Charlie had left Keystone, and one of the funniest farces of the epoch. Later he made a great hit in *Charlie's Aunt.* Sydney Chaplin died in 1965—the first octogenarian in the Chaplin family.

Running one's eye down the list of Chaplin's actors in his earlier films, one sees others who deserve mention, notably *Henry Bergman.* Not only did he play a variety of parts in at least twenty Chaplin films, he also served Chaplin faithfully and magnificently as assistant director. Their collaboration lasted from 1916 up to Bergman's death in 1946. Not least does he deserve to be remembered for his extremely funny female roles (as in *The Rink*). He was an expansive and agreeable actor, with a wide range. Other faithful members of Chaplin's staff were the butler *Albert Austin* (1885–1953), a slender gentleman who originally came from a British vaudeville stage; and the acrobatic *John Rand* (b 1878–d ?), who left Essanay with Chaplin and went over to Mutual, and also much later played parts in his films.

More idiosyncratic was *Leo White* (1887–1949), an English-born actor who began his career in musical comedy, but who abandoned the stage in order to play slippery and cunning types, mostly 'Frenchmen', for Chaplin. More especially he deserves to be remembered for his shady gambler in *The Champion* and his duelling officer in *Carmen.*

However, *Eric Campbell* and *Mack Swain* were more important as actors. The former, with his highly idiosyncratic talent hidden within a gigantic frame, has been especially underrated. To call him to mind one only has to think of the great tough who tyrannises *Easy Street,* bending lamp-posts double with his bare hands. Or the roller-skating gentleman at the spa in *The Cure,* who gets his bandaged foot stuck in the swing doors. For Chaplin. Campbell was a real find. In him he had found his antagonist, his Goliath (Campbell was well over six feet tall) to fight his own little David: a Goliath, what was more, agreeable to acting on the motto that might is right, and ever ready to resort to sheer brutality to prove it. Unlike Mack Swain, Eric Campbell never enjoyed any sympathy from the public. All that went to Charlie! But Eric Campbell plays his villainous roles with great skill. Campbell was of Scottish extraction, and came to Chaplin and Mutual via a job in film journalism in London and a stage appearance in an American musical called *Pom-Pom.* Unfortunately their collaboration was only to last for two brief years. In December 1917 he died in a car accident. Fans will remember him with gratitude in eleven roles, all more or less dastardly.

In vain Chaplin sought to replace him. In 1919 the American

194

press announced that he had engaged an American giant 'Gluff Gluff', a circus artist weighing over 440lb, by the name of Thomas A. Wood. This mastodon, who was to have succeeded Campbell, was however never seen on the silver screen.

If Campbell was a unique figure in his own way, so too was the good-natured giant *Mack Swain*. He had joined Keystone a year earlier than Chaplin and in his many Sennett farces was given the sobriquet Ambrose, because Sennett liked to show him off amid a bevy of his famous bathing beauties. Swain's very finest performance is in *The Gold Rush*, as the starving treasure-hunter who forces Chaplin to serve up one of his boots for dinner. But another delightful memory is his lay worker in *The Pilgrim*. Swain was born in Salt Lake City in 1876 and died in 1935.

Two other names to be remembered, both in connection with Chaplin and as independent farce comedians are *Ben Turpin* and *Chester Conklin*. The former 1894-1940 was engaged by Essanay in 1915, where he was soon spotted by Chaplin, who afterwards played against him in four films. When Turpin had begun his film career his sight was normal; but as the result of an accident he became cross-eyed. And that made his fortune for him. In 1921 he took out a $25,000 insurance policy against his damaged eye becoming well again! Afterwards Turpin joined Mack Sennett with whom he made a remarkable career of his own in full-length films. Like so many others his career was abruptly terminated by the arrival of the talkies—his voice did not suit.

Chester Conklin, known on account of his superb moustache as Walrus, had a good deal more film dealings with Chaplin than Turpin did. During his time with Mack Sennett he played against Chaplin fifteen times, appearing in altogether more than one hundred farces. Conklin began his career as a circus artist, and had begun filming with Sennett in 1913. He appeared sporadically even in his old age, eg, in *The Great Dictator* (1940). Conklin was born in Iowa in 1888 and died at his home in Van Nuys, California, on 11 October 1971. His 83 years made him one of the oldest of the great farce actors. But it was another Chaplin veteran, Hank Mann, born in 1887 and died in a South Pasadena hospital on 25 November 1971, who was to live to be the oldest of all the famous Keystone Cops. He reached the age of 84, and was still appearing in films as late as 1960.

When one considers how swiftly films were made in those days, it is not surprising that Chaplin should at one time or another have played against almost all the old guard of farce comedians:

Turpin, Conklin, Ford Sterling, Fatty Arbuckle, Hank **Mann**, Edgar Kennedy, Slim Summerville, Charlie Chase and Charlie Murray. But it was not until *Limelight* (1952) that he and *Buster Keaton* met in front of the film cameras. By then Buster was in the autumn of his days, as was Snub Pollard, who had also once made so many farces.

Harold Lloyd and Chaplin, on the other hand, never actually came together in a film, though it was touch and go. In 1913 the young Lloyd, tired of not being given any work by his producer, later his friend, Hal Roach, signed up with Sennett. But there were no parts there either. Sennett is said to have had plans to launch him in a big way as a replacement for his star Ford Sterling, who had told him he was going to leave. But the project was abandoned, and Sennett put his money on Chaplin instead—a decision which Sennett seems to have regretted rather more than a year later, when Chaplin too had departed. Certainly he must have done so after Harold had become the great public favourite of the twenties. But not even Mack Sennett could have coped simultaneously with two such major stars as Chaplin and Lloyd. Not that he was unable to cope with most things; Sennett certainly deserved his title the 'king of comedy'. And of course Chaplin's time with this inexhaustible slapstick-maker who had earlier made such famous stars as Mabel Normand, Ford Sterling and Fatty, was of great importance to his career.

Mack Sennett was born in 1880—his real name was Mickall Sinott—and he served his apprenticeship with the famous director David W. Griffith. In 1912 he set up as the lion tamer of the fantastic Keystone cops and in his studios at Edendale outside Los Angeles began to produce an endless series of short farces, in which situation and sensation followed rapidly on each other's heels. In all, Sennett produced (even if he did not in every case direct) no fewer than 548 Keystone farces. From his debut in 1908 up to 1935, when he left the industry, he made altogether 1,081 films. He died in 1960.

In the Chaplin films, Sennett did not merely direct, he also played in at least four of them. It was not until his thirteenth film (*Caught in the Rain*) that Chaplin was allowed to direct them on his own. And it was not until film number 20 (*Laughing Gas*) that he definitely took over the reins. *Tillie's Punctured Romance* was Mack Sennett's most ambitious project as a director and had three stars: Chaplin, Mabel Normand and the famous stage actress Marie Dressler.

All in all, Chaplin was independently responsible for seventeen of the Keystone films, shared the direction of four of them with Mabel, and of one with Sennett and Mabel. Sennett, for his part, independently directed seven films and shared the direction once with Mabel and once with Henry 'Pathé' Lehrman. The latter was not only the first to direct Chaplin (in his début *Making a Living*) but also took charge of three of his first films. On one occasion—in Chaplin's seventh film, *His Favourite Pastime*—the direction (which has left little trace behind it) went to George Nichols.

Finally, it would be unjust not to mention Chaplin's faithful—and able—cameraman *Rollie Totheroh*. From 1915 onwards Totheroh shot all the Essanay films on his own and then went with Chaplin to Mutual. Thereafter—with a certain amount of assistance—he shot all Chaplin's films, up to *Monsieur Verdoux* (1947). For thirty-two years—it is claimed without the least friction!—he collaborated with Chaplin. A minor miracle!

Of Chaplin's eighty-one films, most (sixty-two) were shot during the four years he worked for Keystone, Essanay and Mutual. The figure is remarkable. Yet in sheer energy Chaplin lies far in the wake of his most celebrated competitors. Chaplin has played the lead in only ten full-length films; Harold Lloyd in seventeen; Buster Keaton in thirty; and Laurel and Hardy in twenty-four. Even in total output Chaplin is outdone by Keaton, who played in 122 films, eighty-three of which in the leading role; also by Harold Lloyd, who besides 113 films in his own name had time to make fifty-two as Lonesome Luke, and some fifty as Willie Work. Laurel and Hardy played together in ninety-five films, of which seventy-one were short farces, but individually already had some fifty farce parts to their credit.

Anyone who studies the films Chaplin made during his various periods with Keystone, Essanay and Mutual will find that he gathered around him a little élite troupe, which was kept fairly intact within each company. Often each actor was gifted for more or less one type of role. One became a specialist in butlers, another in old men, a third in shady characters. The leading lady was always melting and sometimes a trifle overblown (with the exception of Mabel Normand). Part of the charm of these old Chaplin films, indeed, lies in recognising their figures, whose typical gesticulations we follow from film to film.

At the same time it must be said that very few indeed were afterwards able to become stars by their own unaided strength—they were too dependent on the master and his surroundings. One who did succeed, however, was Gloria Swanson, later a world-famous vamp and comedienne. Two others were Agnes Ayres and the seductive platinum blonde Jean Harlow. With Chaplin, however, none of these actresses ever had anything more important than an occasional extra role.

Mabel Normand I have mentioned already—she too reached the heights on her own. So, to some extent, did Marie Dressler. But with the exception of Fatty Arbuckle and Ben Turpin, who became stars in their own right, we have to move forward to the year 1923 to come across a future star—in the person of Adolphe Menjou (*A Woman of Paris*). The next star is Paulette Goddard, who after her divorce from Chaplin made her own successful career as a stage comedienne. When he played in *The Great Dictator* (1940), Jack Oakie was already a name in films but can hardly be said to have been a star; and Martha Raye (*Monsieur Verdoux*) was of the same quality.

Limelight starred the well-known British Old Vic actress Claire Bloom. Her role with Chaplin gave her career a further push upwards, but she hardly reached the altitude of such a really great star as Buster Keaton who also appears in the same film. When she was engaged for *A King in New York* Dawn Addams, too, had a name. But she cannot be said to have reached the heights. Not until his last film (hitherto), *A Countess from Hong Kong,* did Chaplin bring two really big guns into action, namely Sophia Loren and Marlon Brando. The effect, even so, was a squib.

How his best and most faithful colleagues accompanied him along his career can be seen from the following table. It is divided into the Keystone period (1914), the Essanay period (1915–February 1916), the Mutual period (March 1916–December 1917), the First National period (1918–February 1923), and Later Films (1923–1967). The figures show how many Chaplin films each actor played in.

My list, I should stress, makes no claim to completeness, especially since such additions as I have been able to make chiefly concern major roles. Though the actors listed certainly also played insignificant extra roles, it has proved impossible to identify them. Even concerning some of their major ones opinions have diverged, owing to the shortcomings of such credits as are still extant.

	Keystone	Essanay	Mutual	First National	Later	Total
Edna Purviance		14	11	9	1	35
Leo White	1	14	5		1	21
John Rand		5	10	3	3	21
Henry Bergman			7	8	5	20
Albert Austin		1	12	5	1	19
Mack Swain	13			3	1	17
Chester Conklin	15				2	17
James T. Kelly		3	10	1		14
Bud Jamison		13		1		14
Frank J. Coleman		4	10			14
Phyllis Allen	8	1	1	3		13
Loyal Underwood			5	7	1	13
Minta Durfee	11					11
Mabel Normand	11					11
Eric Campbell			11			11
Lloyd Bacon		5	6			11
Harry McCoy	11					11
Billy Armstrong		11				11
Fritz Schade	10					10
Edgar Kennedy	10					10
Hank Mann	6				3	9
Alice Davenport	9					9
Charlie Chase	8					8
Charlotte Mineau		2	6			8
Wesley Ruggles		6	2			8
Al St John	7					7
Alice Howell	7					7
Cecile Arnold	7					7
Paddy McGuire		7				7
Slim Summerville	6					6
Fatty Arbuckle	6					6
Norma Nichols	6					6
Fred Goodwins		6				6
Tom Wilson					6	6

Costumes and Types

Chaplin, the little tramp with the tight jacket, the bowler, the walking stick and the outsize shoes has become a legend. We are apt to forget that his genius has flowered in many guises, that he has worn many outfits, and that his outward attributes have varied much more widely than those of, for instance, Laurel and Hardy, or even Lloyd and Keaton. In more than a score of his films he deviates to a greater or lesser extent from his typical tramp role.

In his first film he appears in a rather unsuccessful top hat and morning coat. But even after his second film (*Kid Auto Races at Venice*) had provided him by chance with his classic outfit, he did not rigidly stick to it. In his sixth film, *Tango Tangles*, he appears in normal costume and without the moustache; and in *Mabel at the Wheel*, his first two-reeler, the top hat and morning coat reappear as suitable attributes for a shady character. It is in this film that Chaplin plays the real villain and saboteur.

Throughout *A Busy Day* he plays a woman. Later transvestite guest performances are to be found in *The Masquerader* and *A Woman*. In *The Rounders, A Night in the Show* and *One AM* he jettisons the formal attire, and during his first years we see him as a boxing referee (*The Knockout*), a baker (*Dough and Dynamite*) and a cave man (*His Prehistoric Past*)—though here the bowler in the last and introductory scenes is reminiscent of the tramp.

In *Carmen* he is a fiery lieutenant given to duelling, in *The Adventurer* a convict and an elegantly dressed gentleman, in *Shoulder Arms* a soldier, and in *The Pilgrim* a bogus minister of religion. Though underneath all his guises we can see Charlie the Tramp, he actually presents us with a variegated portrait gallery.

Three times in his career he has played distinct double roles, apart from his 'transformation acts' and dream roles. The first time was in *A Night in the Show* (1915) where he is both a drunken gentleman in the stalls and an equally inebriated hobo in the gods. The second time was in *The Idle Class* (1915), where he plays Edna Purviance's cold-blooded *bon viveur* of a husband, and also the big-hearted but not exactly trustworthy vagabond. Finally, in 1940, in *The Great Dictator*, he is the Jewish barber and the parody of Hitler.

If we look a little more closely at Chaplin's earlier films we shall not find it hard to distinguish certain central settings and behaviour patterns. Of the settings, *one* was certainly dictated by economic considerations—the park. Mack Sennett was loath to waste money on unnecessary sets and props, and having the leafy groves and the lake of Westlake Park so conveniently close to his studios he exploited it to the utmost. On its gravel paths and among its hedges the most surprising encounters took place, often between a policeman and a loving couple in trouble. Many actors either fell or were pushed into 'The Echo Lake' as a climax of some minimal action. Park bench romances and love in the bushes had to provide the inspiration for the controversies and man-hunts which were needed to keep the whole thing going. And it was always Chaplin, with his expressive grimaces, who led these lively walks in the park. The chief park films are *Twenty Minutes of Love, Recreation, Those Love Pangs, Getting Acquainted* and *In the Park*; but the setting was also used in *Caught in the Rain, His Trysting Place* and *Tillie's Punctured Romance*.

Another category in Chaplin's early output was the 'car' film. They were certainly influenced by Mack Sennett's fortunate experiences with wild motor chases in his Keystone Cops farces, using Mabel Normand, Fatty and Ford Sterling, etc. Thus it was only natural that Chaplin, at the outset, should have been flung into a motor race (*Kid Auto Races at Venice*). But the most striking setting of this kind is in *Mabel at the Wheel*, whose whole action takes place on a dirt track. *Mabel's Busy Day, Gentlemen of Nerve,* and to some extent *The Jitney Elopement* are also associated with motoring exploits.

However primitive their humour and however technically crude, Chaplin's films from 1914 and 1915 provide latter-day audiences with authentic and exceedingly interesting interiors from the film studios, variety saloons and cinemas of those days.

Film shootings and all their props and settings can be seen in *A Film Johnny*; but above all in the three films *The Masquerader, His New Job* and the somewhat later *Behind the Screen. The Property Man* and *A Night in the Show* capture milieux drawn from Chaplin's time with Fred Karno. The last of these, a two-reeler, is virtually taken from the very show (*A Night in an English Music Hall*) in which Chaplin was discovered by the film people. And *Tillie's Punctured Romance* offers a perfect cinema interior, 1914-style.

Many people have reacted against the drunken scenes which are not merely episodes in, but also basic to, the action of so many early Chaplin films. In *The Rounders* (with Fatty), in *A Night Out* (Ben Turpin), and in *Pay Day* (also Turpin) Chaplin goes on sprees with a drinking partner. And in *His Favourite Pastime, Mabel's Married Life, The Face on the Bar Room Floor, A Night in the Show* and *One AM* etc, he appears in a more or less inebriated state, while in *The Cure* he is the leader of alcoholic orgies in which the spa patients more or less involuntarily but nonetheless merrily join in.

The Charlie of the first period was aggressive and by no means always sympathetic—still less chivalrous—to the fair sex; and in the heat of the fray he was not infrequently even capable of launching a well-aimed brick at its representatives. That he was an acrobat of the first order there is no question; and when he came to Keystone with its other 'death-daring' actors, he became their teacher in the art of falling without hurting themselves—in this respect only Ben Turpin could compete with this newcomer from Karno's school.

But most astounding of all are Chaplin's insights into the noble art of self-defence. He has a notable eye for the subtler refinements of the ring. Despite the parody, the camera work is superb. When it comes to a struggle at close quarters, both in the ring and out of it, the swiftness of his reactions is superb. Hardly any film comedian of rank, either before or since, has been spared a bout in the ring. But none—not even Buster Keaton—has so elaborately parodied professional boxing or so brilliantly captured its ridiculous aspects as Chaplin did in *The Champion* and, later, in the boxing episode of *City Lights*.

That Chaplin was equally light on his toes in other sports was something to which his close friend Douglas Fairbanks Sr, among others, has testified. Physical exercises were a part of their friendship, and it was by no means the lithe little Chaplin who came off worst. Once, we are told, Douglas, a phenomenon of physical fitness, challenged Chaplin to a race around Pickfair, Doug and Mary Pickford's magnificent park. At first Chaplin lay far in the rear; but in the end Douglas, utterly out of breath, saw himself overtaken by his light-footed and resilient competitor. Charlie Chaplin has had plenty of fight in him—a quality for which, over the years, he has had plenty of use.

Footages and Running Times

Down the decades many Chaplin experts have discussed his films' original footages, with widely differing results. Where films from his Mutual (1916–17) period are concerned, we can rely absolutely on the figures given by the American Chaplin connoisseur, Theodore Huff. Generally speaking, his footages for the silents are somewhat shorter than those given by the respected French expert Jean Mitry. The explanation is simple. The French copies ran to more eloquent and bulky titles than the American or British versions. And this of course made them longer.

A shortcoming has been that we have no exact lengths for the thirty-five Keystone (Mack Sennett) films from 1914, and the fifteen Essanay films (1915–1916) have only been given in terms of reels (a reel is usually about 900ft), for the simple reason that no real footages, it seems, were ever noted down.

If reliable information in this respect is available, even so, it is thanks to the admirable and unique Swedish 'accounting' system, as applied by the Swedish Board of Film Censors. The Danish Statens Filmcensur was almost equally efficient. From 1915 onwards—and even, in one instance, earlier—a card register was kept, with a note of the footages (before cutting) of all Chaplin films handed in for viewing. The Danes too kept their register (after cutting). Unfortunately the Danish censors' films were destroyed in a fire as a result of sabotage during World War II. Their registrations, however, had already been reproduced in the literature.

Even if—as we have seen—certain less scrupulous importers intervened and now and again offered audiences a second-grade product, we have the best reason to suppose that most copies arriving in Sweden in those days, often direct from Keystone and Essanay, were of original length. In the earliest years such gross cuts as afterwards occurred and truncated the films had not yet begun to be made. This can be seen from the footages themselves.

Except for the five films (*A Busy Day, Cruel Cruel Love, Her Friend the Bandit, Recreation* and *The Bond*) never imported into

Sweden, one can find answers at all points by toothcombing Statens Biografbyrå's archives, to which the present writer has been given full access.

Where these five films are concerned I have had the assistance of Denmark's and one of the world's greatest Chaplin experts, namely the late Karl J. Christensen of Copenhagen, and similarly for some Danish copies which turn out to be even a little longer than the Swedish copies. This has made it possible to determine the footages (in metres) for the *whole* of Chaplin's output. Once again it should be pointed out that the figures can never be *exact*, if only because, far into the later silent epoch, films were measured in Sweden as including the leaders, which naturally took up some metres over and above the actual film.

In my list (see Tables and Summaries) I have registered not only the footages (in metres and feet) archived in Sweden—the figure in brackets being for Denmark in those cases where the Danish films were longer—but also the 'official' footages from the Mutual period 1916–17 onwards, as established by Theodore Huff, whose factual information about Chaplin seems the most reliable. The figures given by the Frenchman Mitry, where they diverge from Huff's, are shown in brackets.

Oddly, some Chaplin films from the Mutual series onwards have somewhat higher footages in their Swedish and Danish copies than in their 'official' registrations. With or without leaders, this is simply a fact we must note.

This source of uncertainty has led me, for all footages from the Mutual period onwards (beginning with *The Floorwalker*, 1916) to adhere to Theodore Huff's figures, and only in two cases (*One AM* and *The Count*) to rely on Jean Mitry's, where Huff does not give any.

But what was the playing time of a Chaplin film? This is a more complicated problem. From the turn of the century a silent was designed to run at a rate of sixteen frames a second. However, in the early days there were no mechanically operated projectors and the projectionist, operating it by hand, could not always keep up the steady speed. Towards the end of the first decade of the century, however, a great many cinemas had acquired mechanically driven projectors, and according to the unanimous statements of veterans of the projection room films were then run at eighteen frames a second. In the 1920s the speed even rose to about twenty.

Not until the arrival of the talkies can we speak of a constant number of frames per second. For practical and mechanical reasons it was then fixed at twenty-four. In the following table of the footages and playing times of Chaplin films I have therefore given playing times for the Keystone, Essanay and Mutual films (1914–18) at speeds of 16 and 24fr/sec and if I have included the latter speed it is because, for technical reasons, all revivals of silents must today be run at a speed of 24fr/sec, and on TV even at 25. The reader will thus gain some idea of how far they diverge from the original speed.

From 1918 onwards the playing times are valid for a speed of 18fr/sec (plus a comparative 24fr/sec), up to and including *The Circus* (1928), and thereafter only at 24fr/sec.

For lack of any international figures, the Keystone and Essanay footages (1914–16) have been based on the copies imported into Sweden, or Denmark where they were longer. From the Mutual series onwards, the playing times are based on the accepted international footage, whose chief advocate is Theodore Huff. The footages and playing times of Chaplin's films are to be seen in the following table. As guidance to collectors of Chaplin films in 8mm or 16mm, it should be said that the footage ratio between 8mm, 16mm and 35mm (the figures in the table being for 35mm) is 1 : 2 : 5, ie 5 metres (16.4ft) of 35mm contain as many frames as 2m (6.56ft) of 16mm or 1m (3.28ft) of 8mm (standard eight).

| | | | LENGTH in metres and feet | | | | Playing Time* | |
	ORIGINAL TITLE	FIRST NIGHT	Official		Swedish copy (Danish)		16fr/sec	24fr/sec
			m	*ft*	*m*	*ft*		
1	*Making a Living* (1 reel)	2/2/14	—	—	290	951	15.53	10.35
2	*Kid Auto Races at Venice* (split reel)	7/2/14	—	—	189 (204)	620 (669)	11.10	7.27
3	*Mabel's Strange Predicament* (1 reel)	9/2/14	—	—	257 (314)	843 (1.030)	17.12	11.28
4	*Between Showers* (1 reel)	28/2/14	—	—	263 (270)	863 (886)	14.47	9.51
5	*A Film Johnnie* (1 reel)	2/3/14	—	—	271 (279)	889 (915)	15.17	10.11
6	*Tango Tangles* (1 reel)	9/3/14	—	—	214	702	11.43	7.49
7	*His Favourite Pastime* (1 reel)	16/3/14	—	—	284 (288)	931 (945)	15.46	10.31
8	*Cruel, Cruel Love* (1 reel)	26/3/14	—	—	— (293)	— (961)	16.03	10.42
9	*The Star Boarder* (1 reel)	4/4/14	—	—	290 (292)	951 (958)	16.00	10.40
10	*Mabel at the Wheel* (2 reel)	18/4/14	—	—	593 (611)	1.945 (2.004)	33.28	22.19

	Original Title	First Night	Official		Swedish copy (Danish)		Playing Time* 16fr/sec	24fr/sec
11	*Twenty Minutes of Love* (1 reel)	20/4/14	—	—	293	961	16.03	10.42
12	*Caught in a Cabaret* (2 reel)	27/4/14	—	—	597 (600)	1.958 (1.968)	32.52	21.55
13	*Caught in the Rain* (1 reel)	4/5/14	—	—	300	984	16.26	10.57
14	*A Busy Day* (split reel)	7/5/14			111†	364	6.05	4.03
15	*The Fatal Mallet* (1 reel)	1/6/14	—	—	243 (324)	797 (1.063)	17.45	11.50
16	*Her Friend the Bandit* (1 reel)	4/6/14	—	—	— (303)	— (993)	16.36	11.04
17	*The Knockout* (2 reel)	11/6/14	—	—	485	1.591	26.34	17.43
18	*Mabel's Busy Day* (1 reel)	13/6/14	—	—	285 (289)	935 (948)	15.50	10.33
19	*Mabel's Married Life* (1 reel)	20/6/14	—	—	311	1.020	17.02	11.21
20	*Laughing Gas* (1 reel)	9/7/14	—	—	299	981	16.23	10.55
21	*The Property Man* (2 reel)	1/8/14	—	—	552 (565)	1.811 (1.853)	30.57	20.38
			m	*ft*	*m*	*ft*		
22	*The Face on the Bar Room Floor* (1 reel)	10/8/14	—	—	265	869	14.31	9.41
23	*Recreation* (split reel)	13/8/14	—	—	— (133)	— (426)	7.17	4.52
24	*The Masquerader* (1 reel)	27/8/14	—	—	295	968	16.10	10.46
25	*His New Profession* (1 reel)	31/8/14	—	—	287 (296)	941 (971)	16.13	10.48
26	*The Rounders* (1 reel)	7/9/14	—	—	296	971	16.13	10.48
27	*The New Janitor* (1 reel)	24/9/14	—	—	261 (300)	856 (984)	16.26	10.57
28	*Those Love Pangs* (1 reel)	10/10/14	—	—	297	974	16.16	10.51
29	*Dough and Dynamite* (2 reel)	26/10/14	—	—	613	2.010	33.35	22.23
30	*Gentlemen of Nerve* (1 reel)	29/10/14	—	—	293	961	16.03	10.42
31	*His Musical Career* (1 reel)	7/11/14	—	—	300	984	16.26	10.57
32	*His Trysting Place* (2 reel)	9/11/14	—	—	583	1.912	31.56	21.18
33	*Tillie's Punctured Romance* (6 reel)	14/11/14	—	—	1.462‡	4.796	1.20.08	53.23
34	*Getting Acquainted* (1 reel)	5/12/14	—	—	281 (290)	922 (951)	15.53	10.35
35	*His Prehistoric Past* (2 reel)	7/12/14	—	—	593	1.945	32.29	21.40
36	*His New Job* (2 reel)	1/2/15	—	—	578 (586)	1.896 (1.922)	32.06	21.24

		LENGTH in metres and feet				Playing Time*	
ORIGINAL TITLE	FIRST NIGHT	Official		Swedish copy (Danish)		16fr/sec	24fr/sec
37 A Night Out (2 reel)	15/2/15	—	—	566 (595)	1.856 (1.951)	32.36	·21.43
38 The Champion (2 reel)	11/3/15	—	—	591	1.938	32.23	21.35
39 In the Park (1 reel)	18/3/15	—	—	300	984	16.26	10.57
40 The Jitney Elopement (2 reel)	1/4/15	—	—	597	1.958	32.42	21.48
41 The Tramp (2 reel)	11/4/15	—	—	578	1.896	31.40	21.07
42 By the Sea (1 reel)	29/4/15	—	—	296	971	16.13	10.49
43 Work 2 reel)	21/6/15	—	—	615	2.017	33.42	22.28
44 A Woman (2 reel)	12/7/15	—	—	545	1.788	29.52	19.54
		m	ft	m	ft		
45 The Bank (2 reel)	9/8/15	—	—	605	1.985	33.09	22.06
46 Shanghaied (2 reel)	4/10/15	—	—	540	1.771	29.35	19.43
47 A Night in the Show (2 reel)	20/11/15	—	—	529	1.735	28.59	19.19
48 Carmen (4 reel)	22/4/16	—	—	1.215	3.986	1.06.34	44.23
49 Police (2 reel)	27/3/16	—	—	625	2.050	34.14	22.50
50 Triple Trouble (2 reel) (With footage from 1915)	11/8/18	—	—	445	1.460	20.40	16.15
51 The Floorwalker (2 reel)	15/5/16	528** (560)	1.734 (1.837)	606	1.988	28.56	19.17
52 The Fireman (2 reel)	12/6/16	585 (595)	1.921 (1.952)	632	2.073	32.03	21.22
53 The Vagabond (2 reel)	10/7/16	596 (625)	1.956 (2.050)	642	2.106	32.39	21.46
54 One AM (2 reel)	7/8/16	— (620)	— (2.034)	601 (625)	1.971 (2.050)	33.58	22.39
55 The Count (2 reel)	4/9/16	— (615)	— (2.017)	595 (645)	1.952 (2.116)	33.42	22.28
56 The Pawnshop (2 reel)	2/10/16	591 (620)	1.940 (2.034)	637	2.090	32.23	21.35
57 Behind the Screen (2 reel)	13/11/16	547 (574)	1.796 (1.883)	565	1.853	29.58	19.59
58 The Rink (2 reel)	4/12/16	573 (600)	1.881 (1.968)	615	2.017	31.23	20.56
59 Easy Street (2 reel)	22/1/17	535 (620)	1.757 (2.034)	541 (575)	1.775 (1.886)	29.19	19.32
60 The Cure (2 reel)	16/4/17	559 (590)	1.834 (1.935)	610	2.001	30.38	20.25
61 The Immigrant (2 reel)	17/6/17	551 (584)	1.809 (1.916)	630	2.067	30.11	20.08

		LENGTH in metres and feet				Playing Time*	
ORIGINAL TITLE	FIRST NIGHT	Official		Swedish copy (Danish)		16fr/sec	24fr/sec
62 *The Adventurer* (2 reel)	23/10/17	562 (590)	1.845 (1.935)	632	2.073	30.47	20.32
63 *A Dog's Life* (3 reel)	14/4/18	815 (860)	2.674 (2.820)	775 (785)	2.542 (2.575)	39.41††	29.46
64 *The Bond* (split reel) (Made for US War Bonds)	Autumn 1918	—	—	209¶	685	10.11	7.38
65 *Shoulder Arms* (3 reel)	20/10/18	*m* 958 (1.005)	*ft* 3.142 (3.296)	*m* 908	*ft* 2.978	46.40	35.00
66 *Sunnyside* (3 reel)	15/6/19	844 (890)	2.769 (2.920)	823	2.700	41.06	30.50
67 *A Day's Pleasure* (2 reel)	7/12/19	522 (550)	1.714 (1.804)	513	1.683	25.25	19.04
68 *The Kid* (6 reel)	6/2/21	1.614 (1.700)	5.300 (5.577)	1.551	4.924	1.18.36	58.57
69 *The Idle Class* (2 reel)	25/9/21	584 (615)	1.916 (2.017)	595	1.952	28.27	21.20
70 *Pay Day* (2 reel)	2/4/22	577 (610)	1.892 (2.001)	592	1.942	28.06	21.05
71 *The Pilgrim* (4 reel)	25/2/23	1.219 (1.300)	4.000 (4.265)	1.081	3.546	59.21	44.32
72 *A Woman of Paris* (8 reel)	1/10/23	2.309 (2.450)	7.577 (8.038)	2.119	6.952	1.52.34	1.24.20
73 *The Gold Rush* (9 reel)	16/8/25	2.590 (2.720)	8.498 (8.924)	2.444	8.018	2.06.08	1.34.36
74 *The Circus* (7 reel)	7/1/28	2.042 (2.144)	6.700 (7.034)	1.974	6.476	1.39.26	1.14.35
75 *City Lights* (9 reel)	6/2/31	2.382 (2.380)	7.815 (7.808)	2.405	7.890	—	1.26.56
76 *Modern Times* (9 reel)	5/2/36	2.327 (2.320)	7.634 (7.611)	2.480	8.136	—	1.24.45
77 *The Great Dictator* (12 reel)	15/10/40	3.450 (3.420)	11.319 (11.220)	3.420	11.220	—	2.04.55
78 *Monsieur Verdoux* (12 reel)	11/4/47	3.341	10.961	3.385	11.105	—	2.02.02
79 *Limelight* (13 reel)	23/10/52	3.825	12.549	3.825	12.549	—	2.19.43
80 *A King in New York* (11 reel)	12/9/57	3.015	9.891	3.055	10.023	—	1.50.08
81 *A Countess from Hong Kong* (12 reel)	2/1/67	3.363	11.033	3.015	9.891	—	2.02.50

* Footages are given both for a speed of 16 frames per second, from 1918 onwards, and for 24 frames per second. From the first talkie onwards only 24 frames per second.

† A copy in 8mm in the author's possession. The length re-counted to 35mm copy.

‡ The longest copy shown in Sweden (1969) of *Tillie's Punctured Romance* measured 6,709ft edited for running at 24 frames per second. A silent copy of equivalent length, run at the then normal speed of 16 frames per second would have been 4,472ft, ie, about the same length as the first copy which arrived in Sweden in 1919 and was totally banned.

** The upper line shows the lengths given by the American Chaplin expert Theodore Huff. The figures in brackets are those of the French expert Jean Mitry.

†† This and following films calculated in 18 frames per second.

¶ An 8mm copy in the author's possession. The length re-counted to 35mm copy.

Bibliography

WILLIAM CAHN *The Laugh Makers*, 1957
CHARLES CHAPLIN *My Autobiography*, 1964
CHARLES CHAPLIN JR *My Father, Charlie Chaplin*, 1960
PETER COTES & THELMA NIKLAUS *The Little Fellow*, 1951
THEODORE HUFF *Charlie Chaplin*, 1952
THEODORE HUFF *The Early Work of Charlie Chaplin*, 1945
LEWIS JACOBS *The Rise of the American Film*, New York, 1939
KALTON C. LAHUE *World of Laughter*, Norman, Oklahoma, 1966
KALTON C. LAHUE & TERRY BREWER *Kops and Custards*, Norman, Oklahoma, 1967
PIERRE LEPROHON *Charles Chaplin*. Les nouvelles éditions debresse, Paris, 1957
GERALD D. McDONALD, MICHAEL CONWAY & MARC RICCI *The Films of Charlie Chaplin*, New York, 1965
JEAN MITRY *Image et son, Paris*, Numero Special, Les Films de Ch. Chaplin, 1957
JOHN MONTGOMERY *Comedy Films*, 1954
ROBERT PAYNE *The Great Charlie*, 1957
ISABEL QUIGLY *Charlie Chaplin Early Comedies*, 1968
TERRY RAMSAYE *A Million and One Nights*, New York, 1926
CARLYLE R. ROBINSON *The Private Life of Charlie Chaplin*, Great Stars of Hollywood's Golden Age, New York, 1966
MACK SENNETT *Father Goose*, New York, 1934
MACK SENNETT *King of Comedy*, 1955
GEORGES SADOUL *Vie de Charlot*, Paris, 1952
DAVIDE TURCONI *Mack Sennett*, Rome, 1961
EDWARD WAGENKNECHT *The Movies in the Age of Innocence*, Norman, Oklahoma, 1962
RUNE WALDEKRANZ *Filmen växer upp*, Stockholm, 1941

Filmbladet, years 1915–1922
Filmjournalen, years 1919–1951
Filmen, years 1918–1920
Archives of the Swedish Censor (Statens Biografbyrå)

Index

People

211

212

213

Film Titles